# Sweet & Vicious

# Sweet & Vicious

## Baking with Attitude

### Libbie Summers

Photography by Chia Chong

RIZZOLI
NEW YORK

New York · Paris · London · Milan

*For Joshua.*
*You make my world a sweeter and sweatier place to be.*

The. Best. Ever. Red. Velvet. Cake. is on page 58

# This cookbook is based on a true story.

(Sugar Angel)

"Betty Crocker was a bore," she said. I never had the heart to tell her that Betty wasn't a real person. I just giggled since I knew baking really wasn't Grandma's strong suit, and she had no room to put even a faux Betty down. Her statement must have resonated with me because the last thing I ever wanted to be was a bore—in or out of the kitchen. I wanted to cook with attitude. My style of cooking may have started down home, but it left home at eighteen and never looked back.

My first book, *The Whole Hog Cookbook,* was a fearless take on pork. In it, I cooked up the most inspired and delicious recipes for pig I could imagine. I tried to cover all the basics for cooking pork in a new, fun, and creative way—and that's what I want to do in this book for baking. For many years, I worked as a chef on private yachts, and I prided myself on what I could turn out of the galley under the most extreme conditions. Baking on the high seas surrounded by unruly guests taught me to be inventive and daring. Imagine being in a kitchen space the size of a walk-in closet. Now turn that closet on its side and shake it. Then add a rich guy whom you just met, who is sitting in your living room wearing nothing but a Speedo and demanding carrot cake. What do you do? If you are a cook with chutzpah, you don't just bake the guy a basic carrot cake. You do what I did and make him an over-the-top Habañero Carrot Cake (page 32) with a side of piping hot espresso—hoping upon hope that he loves the hot flavor twist of the cake and that the espresso spills in all the right places. He did and it did. **So, just what is baking with attitude?**

## Welcome the unexpected:

Layered flavors are the unexpected surprises of these recipes. It's easy to add a hot flavor to a recipe by using something like red pepper flakes or diced jalapeños. But what about adding a sweet-hot flavor with an infused sugar like my Red Pepper Flake Sugar (page 203)—it's a whole new taste experience! In the Secret Weapons chapter, I share simple recipes for homemade infused sugars and extract blends, plus loads of ways to use them.

## Be fearless:

Fearless baking is not being afraid to change the recipes you already love and make them more personal, more provocative—something that your friends will talk about instead of talking about you. But before you make a recipe provocative, you have to make it the best it can be. The Fairground Attraction Cake (page 34) is a combination of the most delicious vanilla cake and buttercream frosting I could create using homemade vanilla sugars and extracts plus the best butter. It's pretty perfect right there, but I take it one step further by adding a carnival of cotton candy on top. A foot-high pile of cotton candy to be exact. Or, check out my Solid Gold Beet Cupcakes (page 42), an uber-moist cake made of golden beets and dusted with gold powder. You have to be fearless to tell your guests they're eating beets for dessert. Right?

## Be inspired:

Inspiration comes in many forms, as you will read about in *Sweet & Vicious*, and I hope you will be inspired to try recipes outside your comfort zone. Sure, it's easy to purchase pre-made bread dough in your grocery freezer section, but haven't you always wanted to try making your own baguette? The Napoleon Bread recipe (page 116) will teach you the trick to making a perfectly crisp baguette crust using your home oven. This bread is so good and so rewarding you'll never want to make a sandwich with anything else. Speaking of inspiration, I hope I can inspire you to try one of the most forgiving doughs around: bagel dough. Boat Bagels with Garlic Bacon Topping (page 122) are so easy you can even make them on a boat, which is where I was living with my husband and ten-year-old son when I was first inspired to make them. They have healing powers. Read the story to find out how.

## Have fun:

Attitude isn't about being snarky or mean; it's about having fun and making your guests and family giggle as they eat your food! A great example of this is the Retired Gingerbread Working Girls (page 182). I started with an intensely flavorful gingerbread cookie dough. Sure I could have made cute little gingerbread girl cutouts, but what was the fun in that? I decided to make an exotic dancer cookie, but a playful one. A dancer past her prime. She has all the flavor, with just a little more girth. She's adorable, she's side-splittingly funny, but, most importantly, she's delicious.

## Be creative:

This takes piles of attitude but it's so easy, especially when you are working with pies. To step outside the usual framework and get someone to love a pie they haven't tried before, you have to be creative! After my first trip to Hawaii many years ago, I fell in love with macadamia nuts and wanted to make a macadamia nut pie instead of a pecan pie that year for Thanksgiving. I worked hard to get the flavor right because I knew it was going to be a tough crowd to please. My creativity paid off because now my Wahini Pie (page 150) with its salty smoothness, is requested every year for the holiday table!

## Don't be shy about being sentimental:

It takes attitude to show a little sincere sappiness in your baking. The Salvation Cinnamon Rolls (page 62) offer just that. Every time I bake these thick rich rolls with their spicy cinnamon filling, and slathered with Caramel Cream Cheese Frosting (page 206) I think about all the wonderful friends I left in North Carolina where I made them the first time for the local Methodist church. I still remember the feelings I experienced in the fellowship hall as I watched folks from the congregation bite into the still warm rolls—some people closing their eyes and making the most delightful groan that I knew only Jesus would understand.

## Charm everyone, including your furry friends:

Baking for pets takes an attitude all its own. However, until I developed these recipes, I wasn't always thrilled by the outcome. Dogs can't tell you why they do or don't like a treat. They either eat it or won't—usually in some showy way that's actually very charming! But trust me: when it comes to dog treats, you'll never worry again about any going uneaten. Miles's Southern Squash Casserole Treats (page 195) have their own charm. The recipe is based on a classic squash casserole recipe of buttery crackers, fresh squash, and cheddar cheese. There's no dog north or south of the Mason Dixon line who wouldn't love these.

## Aside from all the bravado and irreverence that comes with baking with an attitude, know this:

The recipes in *Sweet & Vicious* are melt-in-your-mouth amazing, because the love is in the details and the disposition. I promise you this collection of hands-on, take-no-prisoners, unapologetically scrumptious recipes will liberate your baking from the mundane and the saccharine. No calorie-counting vegans, picky eaters, just-one-bite-for-me, hold-the-sauce readers allowed. These desserts are a joyous celebration of sugar, butter, and flour. All you need to start is an attitude, an appetite, and time in tomorrow's schedule for a workout. Now turn the page and let's have some mouthwatering fun.

**P.S.** Whenever you see this symbol (the orange bike I rode at 10 and still ride at 10+) on a recipe page, take a web ride on over to www.libbiesummers.com, click on the watch tab, and follow the links. There, you'll find a fun accompanying video. Some videos will teach, most will inspire, but I hope all will entertain!

# 1

# cakes

Good & Plenty Cupcakes | Salty Pumpkin Spice Cake

Upside-Down Skillet Corn Cake | Girly-Girl Lavender Cake

Habañero Carrot Cake | Fairground Attraction Cake

Hot & Heavy Baby Cakes with Kiss Me Frosting

No Hassle Hoff Cake | Looking for Mr. Goodbar Cake

Coconut Fluff Cake with Guava Buttercream Frosting

Solid Gold Beet Cupcakes | Hog Heaven Chocolate Cake

Bridge & Tunnel Cheesecake | Stoned & Grilled Cornmeal Cake | Lemonhead Cake

Spice Channel Cake | Virgin Cake (*Warning: Gluten Free*) | Chocolate Mug Cakes

Sunday Morning Panettone Muffins | The. Best. Ever. Red. Velvet. Cake.

*I'm a firm believer in keeping most cakes at room temperature. I like to cover my cakes with a cake dome (preferably clear so everyone can admire my work), and place it away from any direct heat. Most cakes will keep for up to five days. If I run out of cake domes, I'll store a cake in my microwave. God knows, I rarely use it for cooking, so at least it's good for something.*

Opposite: Hot & Heavy Baby Cakes with Kiss Me Frosting, page 36

# How to Frost a Layer Cake

**1** If you plan on frosting a lot of cakes, a decorating turntable is a great tool to have; you can also use a cake pedestal or flat plate.

**2** Start by using a serrated knife to slice off the domed top or "crown"of each cake layer (make sure to save the scraps for Cake Scrap Cookies, page 168) so the cake tops are level.

**3** Place a dab of frosting in the center of the turntable or cake pedestal (this acts as a glue to keep the cake in place).

**4** Cut four pieces of waxed paper and place them in a square on the pedestal, leaving space around the dab of frosting (this keeps your pedestal clean). Place the first cake layer in the center of the pedestal on the dab of frosting.

**5** Using an offset spatula and about ½ cup frosting, cover the top of the cake layer. Center the next layer on top of the first. Continue with more layers if the recipe calls for more.

**6** If not, it's time to apply a crumb coat of frosting over the entire cake. A crumb coat is a thin layer of frosting that "seals" the cake (and its crumbs) inside.

**7** Refrigerate the cake for about 30 minutes, then apply the final, decorative layer of frosting: Spread a thick coat over the entire cake.

**8** If you want to make your cake even fancier, use a piping bag and whatever tips you like to pipe on decorative accents, or sprinkle with colored sugar, or top with a figurine of a bride and groom (or groom and groom or bride and bride). Gently pull the waxed paper sheets from under the cake and serve.

## Round Cake

| Big Party, Small Pieces (1" x 2") | | Small Party, Big Pieces (2" x 2") |
|---|---|---|
| 10 | 6" | 8 |
| 28 | 8" | 14 |
| 42 | 10" | 21 |
| 56 | 12" | 28 |
| 82 | 14" | 41 |
| 100 | 16" | 50 |

## Square Cake

| Big Party, Small Pieces (1" x 2") | | Small Party, Big Pieces (2" x 2") |
|---|---|---|
| 18 | 6" | 9 |
| 32 | 8" | 16 |
| 50 | 10" | 25 |
| 72 | 12" | 36 |
| 98 | 14" | 49 |
| 128 | 16" | 64 |

✳

# Good & Plenty Cupcakes

### (star anise–flavored sweet vanilla cake)

yields 20 to 24

Two for the show.

Most American kids wouldn't say black licorice was their favorite candy. German kids, sure. They probably keep a little stash of Katjes-Kinder in the pocket of their lederhosen, but no American kid I ever knew liked black licorice—except for me.

Mom and Dad didn't have a date night very often. Money was tight and Dad was tighter. But, about once a month, they would leave me in the charge of my older sisters and go to a "show" (that's what Midwesterners call a movie).

When allowed, I'd lie on my mom's bed and follow her every move as she got ready for the show. Mom was what people called a natural beauty. Her high cheekbones and olive complexion didn't require all the makeup my friends' mothers wore. I dreamt of the day that I could wear hot pants and tease my hair as high as hers. (I already knew I couldn't wear makeup until I was thirteen. It was a rule she reminded my older sisters of daily—show or no show.)

Show nights held a certain excitement for me—not just because I got to see my parents dressed to the nines and holding hands, and certainly not because I had two older sisters bossing me around all evening. No, the real excitement was in knowing what I would find in the morning, perched on the only clean part of my dresser: Two boxes (not just one!) of my favorite candy, Good & Plenty—pill-shaped, soft black licorice pieces covered in a white or pink candy coating. A treat from my parents—two for the show.

2 ¾ cups cake flour

1 tablespoon baking powder

¾ teaspoon salt

1 ⅔ cups star anise sugar (page 203) or regular sugar

12 tablespoons butter, at room temperature

4 large egg whites, plus 1 whole large egg

1 teaspoon star anise extract (page 198)

1 cup milk

Swiss Meringue Frosting (page 205), tinted hot pink

24 to 48 Good & Plenty candies
(from one 6-ounce box; you'll have extra to snack on)

❶ Preheat the oven to 350° F. Line two standard cupcake pans with paper liners (for 20 to 24 cupcakes).

❷ In the bowl of a standing mixer fitted with the whisk attachment, combine the flour, baking powder, salt, and star anise sugar. Add the butter and mix for 2 minutes, or until thoroughly combined. The mixture may form a paste, depending on how warm the butter is, and that's okay. Add the egg whites one at a time, beating well after each addition. Scrape down the bowl as needed. Beat in the whole egg and the star anise extract. Add the milk in thirds, beating well after each addition. Continue to beat for another 2 minutes, or until the batter is light and fluffy.

❸ Scoop the batter into the cupcake liners, filling the cups three-quarters full. Bake for 20 to 25 minutes, until the cakes are barely golden. Allow to cool completely before frosting them. Garnish with Good & Plenty candies. ✳

\*

# Salty Pumpkin Spice Cake
## (warm caramel frosting + pumpkin seed brittle topping)
### serves 12 to 16

When you say no, say it in such a way that it leaves a lasting impression.

The last interview I had for a mainstream job went on for two hours and twenty-six minutes. It was a big-girl kind of job with a very well-known company, and I was honored to be tapped to interview for the position.

What started out as a pleasant interview by two men and one woman in a professionally decorated boardroom quickly turned into an interrogation. For two hours, I tried to stay calm and answer their questions with honesty and humor. Sometimes I was successful, sometimes not. The last request of the interview (and the only one I remember) was that I name four impressive things about myself. I don't remember the first three answers I gave, but I do remember the last. I described this cake recipe I had been working on at home: two layers of the best pumpkin cake you've ever eaten separated by thick layers of caramel frosting and topped with shards of pumpkin seed brittle. I must have gotten lost in my own thoughts and hunger during the description, because when I opened my eyes there were six eyes staring at me and three mouths wide open. Stunned is how I would describe them.

We exchanged pleasantries as they walked me to the elevator. It didn't take me more than two floors on the descent to realize I'm not cut out to work in a corporate environment. Apparently, they did not feel the same way, as two weeks later I had a formal offer. I was shocked and flattered, but I knew the truth. That night I baked them a Salty Pumpkin Spice Cake and shipped it to their offices overnight, packed securely inside a plastic cake container with a "No, thank you" note attached.

Since that cake shipped two years ago, I've done twenty-four freelance jobs for that company. I think it's safe to say this is one impressive cake!

*continued on page 22*

3 cups all-purpose flour

1 teaspoon salt

½ teaspoon baking soda

1 tablespoon baking powder

¼ teaspoon ground cloves

1 ½ teaspoons ground ginger

1 ½ teaspoons ground cinnamon

Pinch of ground cayenne

1 cup (2 sticks) butter

2 cups packed dark brown sugar

4 large eggs

1 (15-ounce) can pure pumpkin puree

½ cup plain yogurt (nonfat works fine, but I prefer whole Greek yogurt)

1 teaspoon vanilla paste or extract

Caramel Frosting (page 206), still warm

Pumpkin Seed Brittle Topping (recipe follows)

## salty pumpkin spice cake

❶ Preheat the oven to 350° F. Spray two 9-inch round cake pans with nonstick cooking spray and set aside.

❷ In a medium mixing bowl, sift together the flour, salt, baking soda, baking powder, cloves, ginger, cinnamon, and cayenne. Set aside.

❸ In the bowl of a standing mixer fitted with the paddle attachment, cream together the butter and brown sugar on medium speed until fluffy. Reduce the speed to low and add the eggs one at a time, beating until smooth after each addition. Add the pumpkin, yogurt, and vanilla and mix until well combined. Add the flour mixture and mix until combined.

❹ Divide the batter evenly between the prepared baking pans. Bake for 40 minutes, or until the cake begins to pull away from the sides of the pan and a toothpick inserted in the center comes out clean. Let the cakes cool slightly in their pans while you prepare the frosting. It's important to frost the cake while the cake and the frosting are both still warm.

❺ Frost the cake (see "How to Frost a Layer Cake," page 16), using half of the frosting for each layer. (Don't frost the sides.) Garnish with shards of Pumpkin Seed Brittle. (This cake is meant to be sweet and vicious-looking!) Slice and serve. ❋

### Pumpkin Seed Brittle

1 cup sugar

½ cup corn syrup

1 ¾ cups pepitas (raw hulled pumpkin seeds)

1 teaspoon baking soda

2 tablespoons butter

¼ teaspoon ground cinnamon

⅛ teaspoon ground cayenne

Pinch of sea salt

## pumpkin seed brittle topping, yields about 3 cups

❶ Spray a baking sheet with nonstick cooking spray and set aside.

❷ In a large skillet over high heat, stir together the sugar, corn syrup, and ¼ cup water and bring the mixture to a full boil. Stir in the pepitas with a heatproof spatula. Continue to cook for 5 minutes, stirring occasionally, until the syrup becomes thick and honey colored and you begin to smell the pepitas cooking. Remove the skillet from the heat and stir in the baking soda. Working quickly, stir in the butter, cinnamon, and cayenne and continue to stir until the butter has melted. Turn the brittle out onto the prepared baking sheet and, working quickly, use the back of your spatula to spread the mixture out to a thin 8-by-10-inch rectangle. Sprinkle the top with sea salt and let the brittle cool completely, for about 20 minutes, then break into shards. Store the shards in an airtight container until ready to decorate the cake (shards will keep for 10 days). ❋

✳

# Upside-Down Skillet Corn Cake

## (1 batter, 5 different fruits, 5 different cakes)

### each recipe serves 8 to 10

I never used to like upside-down cake because I always thought it had to be made with canned pineapple and maraschino cherries. (For some reason, I was convinced those preternaturally red cherries must cause cancer; then I grew up and realized you can get cancer from just about anything.)

As it turns out, when fresh fruits are used, I am an upside-down-cake craftsman. I mastered the perfect batter and then fine-tuned the fruit bottoms to include my favorite fruits. For a big show (and God knows I love dinner party showmanship), at your next dinner party, try turning one of these upside-down cakes over onto a large cutting board and placing it in the middle of your table for your guests to help themselves. I guarantee no one will miss the maraschino cherries.

## For the fruit layer:

4 tablespoons butter

¾ cup packed light brown sugar

Choice of fruit option (opposite)

## For the cake batter:

1 ¼ cups all-purpose flour

¼ cup fine-ground cornmeal

1 ½ teaspoons baking powder

¼ teaspoon salt

¼ teaspoon freshly grated nutmeg

1 cup (2 sticks) butter, at room temperature

¾ cup sugar

½ teaspoon vanilla paste

2 large eggs, at room temperature

½ cup milk, at room temperature

Vanilla ice cream, for serving

1. **Make the fruit layer:** In a 10-inch cast-iron skillet over medium heat, melt the butter until just bubbling. Add the brown sugar and any other ingredients except the fruit and continue to cook, stirring constantly, until the sugar is completely melted and the mixture begins to bubble. Remove from the heat and let cool slightly. Arrange two layers of the fruit in a decorative pattern to cover the brown sugar mixture in the bottom of the skillet. Set aside while you make the cake batter.

2. **Make the cake batter:** Preheat the oven to 350° F. In a medium mixing bowl, whisk together the flour, cornmeal, baking powder, salt, and nutmeg. Set aside.

3. In the bowl of a standing mixer fitted with the paddle attachment, cream the butter and sugar together until light and fluffy. Add the vanilla paste and beat to combine. Add the eggs one at a time, beating until smooth after each addition. With the mixer on low speed, beat in half of the flour mixture, then add the milk and mix to combine, then add the last of the flour mixture. Mix only until the flour mixture is just incorporated. Spread the batter over the fruit, being careful not to move the fruit around too much. You may smooth the top, but don't worry too much because everything will settle as it bakes.

4. Bake for 45 minutes, until the cake begins to pull away from the sides of the skillet and you can see the syrup bubbling around the sides. The center should feel set to the touch. Carefully remove the skillet from the oven and let cool for 15 to 20 minutes.

5. Run a knife around the edge of the skillet, then very carefully place a plate (much larger than the diameter of the skillet) over the top of the skillet and flip the skillet over to turn the cake out onto the plate. There will be wonderful, oozing syrup escaping around the sides. Serve the cake warm with a scoop of vanilla ice cream. ✳

## Fruit options:

1. ### If making grilled pineapple

   2 tablespoons Gosling's Black Seal Rum

   1 medium pineapple, peeled, cored, sliced ½-inch-thick, and grilled on a hot outdoor grill just until char marks appear (do not turn)

2. ### If making pear *(pictured on page 26)*

   3 firm ripe Bosc pears, peeled, cored, and sliced lengthwise into ¼-inch slices

3. ### If making mango

   2 tablespoons Coconut Rum (I use Malibu Rum; I hate the stuff, but it tastes great in this)

   4 firm ripe mangoes, peeled and sliced lengthwise into thick slices

   ½ cup mango nectar (to replace the whole milk in the cake recipe)

4. ### If making blueberry peach

   5 firm ripe fresh peaches, pitted, peeled, and sliced lengthwise into thick slices

   1½ cups blueberries, folded in just before pouring the batter into the skillet

5. ### If making apricot

   2 tablespoons apricot nectar

   10 to 12 small fresh apricots, sliced in half lengthwise and pitted

I've found an apology baked in the form of a cake is always accepted.

Opposite: Pear Upside-Down Skillet Corn Cake on page 25

\*

# Girly-Girl Lavender Cake

## (vanilla cake studded with fragrant lavender)

serves 20

I put lavender in everything from mashed potatoes and ice cream to homemade marshmallows and this delicious cake. It takes a skilled hand and a lock-tight restraining order on your part not to overdo it. What starts out as a faint floral flavor can quickly turn into something akin to licking grandma's soap if you're not careful. This cake is everything baking with lavender was meant to be: demure, delicious, and darling. A true girly girl.

2 ¾ cups cake flour

1 ⅔ cups sugar

1 tablespoon baking powder

¾ teaspoon salt

1 tablespoon dried lavender buds, crushed

¾ cup (1 ½ sticks) butter, at room temperature

4 large egg whites, plus 1 whole large egg

1 cup unsweetened coconut milk

½ teaspoon S&V House Blend Almond Extract (page 199) or regular almond extract (page 198)

1 teaspoon vanilla extract (page 198)

Lavender Simple Syrup (recipe on page 30) or prepared lavender syrup like Monin brand

Swiss Meringue Buttercream Frosting (page 205), colored purple using purple food coloring

*You may use any decorative pattern for your final layer of frosting. I used a large star tip and, starting from the bottom, covered the cake with simple rosettes. Super girly.*

# Cakes

✳

1. Preheat the oven to 350° F. Spray two 8-inch round cake pans with nonstick cooking spray, line the bottoms with parchment paper, and spray the paper. Set aside.

2. In the bowl of a standing mixer fitted with the paddle attachment, on low speed, combine the flour, sugar, baking powder, salt, and lavender. Add the butter and beat until the mixture has the consistency of fine sand or a paste. Increase speed and add the egg whites one at a time, beating well after each addition, then add the whole egg and beat until thoroughly incorporated. Scrape down the bowl as needed. The batter will be thick.

3. In a liquid measuring cup, stir together the coconut milk, vanilla extract, and almond extract. Pour this mixture into the batter in thirds, beating well after each addition, until the batter is fluffy. Scrape down the sides of the bowl as needed.

4. Divide the batter evenly between the prepared pans and bake for 25 to 35 minutes, until a toothpick inserted in the center comes out clean. Let the cake cool in the pans completely before frosting.

5. Slice a thin layer of cake from the top of each layer to create a flat surface (save the scraps for Cake Scrap Cookies, page 168). Place one layer (cut side up) on a cake pedestal or plate and tuck waxed paper under the edges of the cake to keep the pedestal clean. Using a chopstick or skewer, poke a few holes in the top of the cake. Brush the top of the cake with half of the lavender syrup. Let the syrup seep into the holes. Spread 1 heaping cup of the frosting in a generous layer over the top of the first cake layer. Place the second cake layer on top of the frosting, cut side up, poke holes in the top, and brush with the remaining syrup. Use 1 heaping cup of the frosting to apply a crumb coat (see "How to Frost a Layer Cake," page 16) to cover the entire cake (it's okay if you can see the cake through the frosting). Refrigerate for 30 minutes.

6. Use the remaining frosting (about 3 cups) to apply the final decorative layer to the cake. This is the fun part! Serve immediately. ✳

## Lavender Simple Syrup, yields 1 cup

I'm not really an iced tea drinker, but I did a menu item for a cool Southern store a number of years ago that included a lavender iced tea. I thought it was genius. Give it a try and let me know what you think: Just replace the sugar in your iced tea with the syrup to taste.

1 cup sugar

1 tablespoon lavender extract (page 198)

In a medium saucepan over medium heat, combine the sugar and 1 cup water. Cook, stirring, until the sugar dissolves. Simmer for 5 minutes. Remove from the heat and let cool for at least 30 minutes, then stir in the lavender extract. Store lavender simple syrup in a sterilized bottle (run it through the dishwasher) with a tight-fitting lid in a cool dry place for up to 3 months. ✳

✳

# Habañero Carrot Cake

### (carrot cake with a hint of fire)

serves 20

*Carrot cake is like a shy girl at a high school dance. If you don't do something to spice her up, she has a tendency to be stuck making small talk with the creepy Algebra teacher.*

2 cups all-purpose flour

2 teaspoons baking soda

2 teaspoons baking powder

½ teaspoon salt

2 teaspoons ground cinnamon

⅛ teaspoon ground cloves

Pinch of ground cayenne

Pinch of freshly grated nutmeg

4 large eggs

½ cup granulated sugar

1 cup packed dark brown sugar

1 cup chopped fresh pineapple

½ cup applesauce

¾ cup vegetable oil

1 teaspoon hot pepper extract (page 198)

1 teaspoon vanilla extract (page 198)

4 cups grated carrots (about 10 medium), using the large side of a cheese grater

1 habañero chile, stemmed, seeded, and minced

Cream Cheese Frosting (page 206)

Hot Spiced Pecans (recipe follows)

❶ Preheat the oven to 350° F. Spray two 8-inch square baking pans with nonstick cooking spray and set aside.

❷ In a medium mixing bowl, whisk together the flour, baking soda, baking powder, salt, cinnamon, cloves, cayenne, and nutmeg. Set aside.

❸ In a large mixing bowl, using a hand mixer, or in the bowl of a standing mixer, beat together the eggs, both sugars, pineapple, applesauce, oil, and both extracts until well combined. Gradually add the flour mixture and continue to beat until fully incorporated. Fold in the carrots and chile. Divide the batter between the prepared pans and bake for 25 to 30 minutes, until a toothpick inserted in the center comes out clean. Let cool in the pans completely, then remove the cakes.

❹ Frost the cake (see "How to Frost a Layer Cake," page 16), using 1½ cups of the frosting for the first layer and 1½ cups for the top and sprinkling half of the spiced pecans on the first layer of frosting and the remaining spiced pecans on the top. (I don't frost the sides of this cake because I like the taste to be more spicy than sweet, so I only use 3 cups of the frosting recipe. If you choose to frost the sides of the cake, you'll need the entire recipe of frosting.) Serve immediately. ✳

## Hot Spiced Pecans, yields 2 cups

2 cups chopped pecans

2 teaspoons ground cayenne

2 tablespoons butter, melted

❶ Preheat the oven to 350° F. Line a baking sheet with parchment paper.

❷ Toss the pecans, cayenne, and butter together on the baking sheet and bake for 10 minutes. Let cool completely before using. ✳

# Sweet heat.
## *Wicked good.*

✳

# Fairground Attraction Cake

## (perfect vanilla cake + sweet cotton candy)

serves 20

One memorable day during my twelfth summer, my long fascination with fairground workers began. Carnys had their own music, their own language, and a certain smell that I wouldn't be able to identify until many years later at an Earth, Wind and Fire concert. They were tattooed and toothless, but usually not too terrifying.

"Step right up, little lady. Win a prize," I heard them call as I strolled down the walkways of the midway, a month's worth of babysitting money burning a hole in my pocket. I was a competitive child, but it was not the lure of winning a stuffed animal the size of Utah that intrigued me. It was each carny worker's look that drew me to the games.

Because one worker was wearing overalls and a trucker hat from a state I'd never heard of—Utah—I stood for an hour and sprayed water from a gun to force a toy horse to move down a racetrack.

Because another carny had abnormally long blond hair and a tattoo of Cher (or Marlo Thomas, I'm still not sure) on her left wrist, I threw buckets of softballs at a row of clowns for hours. And when my mom came to collect me as the midway was closing, I was throwing the last of my money in the form of a wooden ring at various-sized square boxes. Why? Because the worker wore a tattered turquoise beret and seemed funny . . . in a two-clowns-short-of-a-circus kind of way.

Over the years, my fairground attraction has never faded. I rarely drive past a carnival without stopping and paying an entrance fee. Not to ride a Ferris wheel or Tilt-A-Whirl, but to eat cotton candy and play games of chance with some of the liveliest people I've ever met.

¾ cup milk

2 teaspoons vanilla paste

12 tablespoons butter, at room temperature, plus 2 tablespoons for the pans

1 ¾ cups vanilla sugar (page 202), plus more for the pans

2 ¾ cups cake flour

1 tablespoon baking powder

½ teaspoon salt

5 large egg whites, at room temperature

Swiss Meringue Frosting (page 205)

1 (3 ounce) bag prepared cotton candy (preferably blue)

# Cakes

*

① In a small saucepan over low heat, stir together the milk and vanilla paste. Bring the mixture to a simmer, then remove from the heat and let cool to room temperature.

② Preheat the oven to 350° F. Butter two 8-inch round cake pans, line the bottoms with parchment paper, and butter the paper. Add 1 to 2 tablespoons vanilla sugar to the pans and swish it around to coat the inside. Set aside.

③ In the bowl of a standing mixer fitted with the paddle attachment, sift together the flour, vanilla sugar, baking powder, and salt. Mix on low speed for 10 seconds, then add the butter and the milk mixture and beat on low speed until combined. Increase the speed to medium and mix for 1 minute.

Add 2 egg whites and beat on medium speed for 30 seconds. Add the remaining 3 egg whites and continue to beat for 30 seconds.

④ Divide the batter between the prepared pans and use an offset spatula to level the top of each. Bake for 25 minutes, or until a toothpick inserted in the center comes out clean. Do not overbake. Let the layers cool in the pans for 10 minutes before turning them out onto a cooling rack. Let cool completely.

⑤ Frost the cake (see "How to Frost a Layer Cake," page 16). Finally, let the carny worker in you come out and decorate the top of the cake with piles of cotton candy—as high as you can get it! ✳

✳

# Hot & Heavy Baby Cakes with Kiss Me Frosting

## (candy-spiced vanilla cake + cinnamon candy frosting)

### yields 4 triple-layer baby cakes | serves 12

Anna is a fireball who works as my assistant. A playful, home-schooled girl with a spicy personality and a lust for a world-schooled life. At seventeen, she finds excitement in the mundane things I take for granted. And she finds beauty in the worst of my castoffs.

Anna sees no evil in the world—her passions are pure. She loves just for the sake of loving, yet she tells me she has never fallen "in love." I can only hope I'm still a part of Anna's life when the right boy finally captivates her.

Until then, I can only use my imagination to fantasize about what it will look like when Anna shares her heart with another . . . red balloons and all.

1 cup buttermilk

2 teaspoons S&V House Blend Almond Extract (page 199) or regular almond extract (page 198)

2 ¾ cups all-purpose flour

1 ⅓ cups sugar

1 tablespoon baking powder

¾ teaspoon salt

12 tablespoons butter, at room temperature

5 large eggs (4 separated, 1 whole)

1 ½ cups crushed Red Hots cinnamon candies, plus more for garnish

1 to 2 Atomic Fire Balls candy, crushed (I use a zip-top bag and a hammer)

Kiss Me Frosting (page 209)

❶ Preheat the oven to 350° F. Line a heavy-duty 13-by-18-inch rimmed baking sheet (a half sheet pan) with parchment paper and set aside.

❷ In a small mixing bowl, whisk together the buttermilk and almond extract. Set aside.

❸ In the bowl of a standing mixer fitted with the whisk attachment, whisk together the flour, sugar, baking powder, and salt on low speed. Add the butter and mix just until a fine crumb forms. If a paste forms instead, that's okay. With the mixer on medium speed, add 4 egg whites one at a time, beating well after each addition. Add the whole egg and beat well. Scrape down the bowl as needed. Add the buttermilk mixture in thirds, beating well after each addition until the batter is fluffy. Scrape down the bowl as needed. Fold in the Red Hots. Pour the batter onto the baking sheet, evenly spread the batter with a spatula, and bake for 30 minutes, or until a toothpick inserted in the center comes out clean. Rotate the baking sheet once halfway through the baking process.

❹ In a small saucepan over low heat, melt the Atomic Fire Balls in ¼ cup water. If you like a spicier syrup, add more crushed fireballs. Remove from the heat and let the syrup cool completely.

❺ Let the cake cool completely in the baking sheet. Using a chopstick or skewer, poke holes in the top of the cake. Lightly brush it with the syrup and let the syrup soak into the cake. Use a 3 ½-inch ring mold to cut 12 cake rounds (each cake will be three layers thick). Frost the cake (see "How to Frost a Layer Cake," page 16; there's no need to slice the top off each layer, of course), using a heaping ¼ cup frosting on the first and second layers and as much frosting as you like on the top. (I don't frost the sides of this cake, but you can if you like.) The frosting is so good you will want to eat it with a spoon! Garnish with an extra cinnamon candy, a paper heart, or a simple kiss. ✳

✳

# No Hassle Hoff Cake

## (hassle-free apple spice cake, streusel topping)

serves 12

This is a delicious no-hassle cake dedicated to the only two things I can say with a German accent: streusel and David Hasselhoff.

### For the cake:

½ cup (1 stick) butter, at room temperature

½ cup sugar

2 large eggs

2 tablespoons milk

1 ¼ cups self-rising flour

1 teaspoon ground cinnamon

¼ teaspoon ground ginger

Pinch of salt

Pinch of freshly ground black pepper

4 Granny Smith apples, peeled, cored, and thinly sliced

### For the streusel topping:

¾ cup self-rising flour

½ cup (1 stick) butter, at room temperature

½ cup packed light brown sugar

½ teaspoon ground cayenne

½ cup chopped pecans

Confectioners' sugar, for dusting

❶ Preheat the oven to 350° F. Spray a 9-inch springform pan with nonstick cooking spray, line the bottom with parchment paper, and spray the paper. Set aside.

❷ In the bowl of a standing mixer fitted with the paddle attachment, cream together the butter and sugar until light and fluffy. Add the eggs one at a time, beating well after each addition. Add the milk and mix. With the mixer on low speed, gradually add the flour, cinnamon, ginger, salt, and pepper.

❸ Spoon the batter into the prepared pan. Arrange the sliced apples in a fan pattern to cover the top of the batter.

❹ Make the streusel topping: Using your hands, mix the flour and butter together until the mixture resembles coarse crumbs. Stir in the brown sugar, cayenne, and pecans.

❺ Sprinkle the topping evenly over the apples. Bake for 1 hour, or until the cake is brown and firm. Remove from the oven and let cool in the pan completely before removing from the pan. Dust with confectioners' sugar, slice, and serve. ✳

✳

# Looking for Mr. Goodbar Cake

### (10 buttery layers, pourable fudge frosting)

#### serves 24

I'm a snob about chocolate until it comes to the guilty pleasure of a Mr. Goodbar. This recipe is an offering to the God of Hershey and all things decadent in this world.

#### For the cake:

3 cups all-purpose flour

¼ teaspoon salt

1¼ teaspoons baking powder

1 cup (2 sticks) butter, at room temperature

2 cups sugar

5 large eggs

1 cup evaporated milk

2 teaspoons vanilla extract (page 198)


#### For the pourable fudge frosting, yields 5 cups:

1 cup (2 sticks) butter

2 (12-ounce) cans evaporated milk

½ teaspoon vanilla extract (page 198)

½ cup unsweetened cocoa powder

6 cups sifted confectioners' sugar


6 (1.75-ounce) Mr. Goodbar candy bars, finely chopped (2 cups)

❶ **Make the cake:** Preheat the oven to 350° F. Spray ten 9-inch round cake pans with nonstick baking spray and set aside (use disposable foil cake pans if you don't have enough pans).

❷ In a medium mixing bowl, whisk together the flour, salt, and baking powder. Set aside.

❸ In the bowl of a standing mixer fitted with the whisk attachment, whisk the butter and sugar together for 3 minutes, or until creamy. With the mixer on low speed, add the eggs one at a time and mix until each is incorporated and the batter is smooth. Scrape down the bowl as needed. Gradually add the flour mixture and mix for 3 minutes, or until fully incorporated. Slowly add the evaporated milk, vanilla extract, and a scant ½ cup water and mix until smooth. Using a heaping ½-cup measure, divide the batter among the 10 baking pans and spread evenly with an offset spatula. Tap the bottoms of the pans on the countertop to evenly distribute the batter.

❹ Put three pans in the middle of the preheated oven and bake for 14 minutes, or until the layers feel firm when pressed in the centers and the cake is beginning to pull away from the sides of the pans. Let cool in the pans. Bake the remaining layers of cake the same way.

**❺ Meanwhile make the pourable fudge frosting:** In a medium saucepan, melt the butter over low heat. Remove the pan from the heat and whisk in the evaporated milk, vanilla, and cocoa powder. Return to the heat and cook for 10 minutes, being careful not to let the mixture boil.

**❻** Remove from the heat and gradually whisk in the confectioners' sugar. Return the pan to medium-low heat and continue to cook, whisking often, for 13 minutes, or until the frosting thickens enough to coat the back of a spoon. Let cool for 30 minutes before you begin to frost the cake. The frosting should still be slightly warm.

**❼** Start assembling the cake as the layers cool. Put the first cake layer on a cake pedestal and spread a thin layer of frosting (a heaping ¼ cup) on top. (The frosting will be runny.) Sprinkle with some of the crushed candy bar. Place the second layer of cake atop the first, spread another thin layer of the frosting on top, and sprinkle with the candy bar pieces. Repeat for each remaining layer of the cake, using most of the crushed candy bar before the final layer is added. Scoop up any frosting that has run down onto the cake pedestal and add to the remaining frosting in the bowl to cover the sides and top of the cake. Top with the rest of the crushed candy. Refrigerate the cake for 30 minutes before serving. ✳

✳

# Coconut Fluff Cake
# with Guava Buttercream Frosting
## (a "Southern" island cake)
### serves 24

I love fresh coconut but, truth be told, I was never a coconut cake lover. Nothing against the cake itself; my aversion was deeply rooted in an intense dislike of that artificially sweetened shredded coconut used far too often by the bakers of my youth. I could never get past the frosting to like the cake—until I had to.

I married a man who was a coconut cake lover, and so began my experiments in baking the perfect coconut cake. I tried to create a recipe that my grandmother would approve of, but that would still be something my husband and I could both sink our teeth into. Something with Caribbean flair. Something exactly like this one.

I am now a coconut cake lover.

2 ½ cups all-purpose flour, sifted

1 tablespoon baking powder

1 teaspoon salt

5 large egg whites

1 ¾ cups sugar

¾ cup vegetable shortening, at room temperature

1 ⅛ cups unsweetened coconut milk (not cream of coconut—save that for piña coladas)

1 teaspoon S&V House Blend Almond Extract (page 199)

½ teaspoon coconut extract

1 tablespoon guava paste, at room temperature

Guava Buttercream Frosting (page 208)

2 cups natural coconut flakes, toasted (see Note)

*To toast coconut flakes, spread them on a baking sheet and toast in a 350° F oven, stirring once or twice, until golden, 3 to 5 minutes. Let cool completely before using.*

❶ Preheat the oven to 350° F. Spray two 9-inch round cake pans with nonstick cooking spray and line the bottoms with parchment paper. Set aside.

❷ In a medium mixing bowl, sift together the flour, baking powder, and salt. Set aside.

❸ In the bowl of a standing mixer fitted with the whisk attachment, whisk the egg whites until soft peaks form. Transfer to a separate bowl and set aside.

❹ Exchange the whisk attachment for the paddle attachment and put the sugar and shortening in the same mixer bowl (no need to clean it). Beat on medium speed for 3 minutes, or until fluffy. With the mixer on low speed, gradually add the flour mixture, alternating with the coconut milk, and beat for 2 minutes, until well combined. Scrape down the bowl as needed. Add the almond and coconut extracts and mix just until combined. Add the egg whites and mix on low just until they are incorporated. The egg whites will deflate a bit.

❺ Divide the batter between the prepared pans and bake for 25 to 30 minutes, until a toothpick inserted in the center comes out clean. Remove from the oven and let the layers cool in the pans for 5 minutes before turning out onto a rack and allowing to cool completely.

❻ In a small bowl, stir together the guava paste and ¼ cup hot water. Don't worry if a few lumps of the guava paste remain. Set aside to cool slightly.

❼ Slice a thin layer of cake from the top of each layer to create a flat surface (save the scraps for Cake Scrap Cookies, page 168). Place one layer (cut side up) on a cake pedestal or plate. Using a chopstick or skewer, poke a few holes in the top of the cake. Brush the top of the cake with half of the guava syrup mixture. Let the syrup seep into the holes.

❽ Spread 1 cup frosting (about a quarter of the recipe) in a generous layer over the top of the first cake layer. Place the second cake layer on top of the frosting, cut side up, poke holes in the top, and brush with the remaining guava syrup. Use 1 cup frosting to apply a crumb coat (see "How to Frost a Layer Cake," page 16) to cover the entire cake (it's okay if you can see the cake through the frosting). Refrigerate for 30 minutes.

❾ Use the remaining frosting (about 2 cups) to apply the final decorative layer to the cake. This is the fun part! Sprinkle the coconut flakes on the top of the cake for garnish. ✽

✳

# Solid Gold Beet Cupcakes

### (yellow beets, candied ginger)

#### yields 12

Doctor. Lawyer. Astronaut. These are the conventional answers given by most kids when asked what they want to be when they grow up. My standard answer was—much to my parents' dismay—a *Solid Gold* dancer.

The *Solid Gold* dancers were everything in the 1980s: bedazzled babes dancing in the background to top recording artists on the television show *Solid Gold.* I watched them with a critical eye each week before attempting their choreography in the privacy of my bedroom. Although I had taken only enough dance classes to fumble clumsily through one recital performance of *Zorba the Greek,* I just knew that dancing was my gift. After all, as I reminded my dance teacher, I wasn't Greek.

I never became a *Solid Gold* dancer. Life and a gift for athletics led me in a different direction. But when I'm on a wedding dance floor and the DJ cues up "Gloria," I can still bust out a move or two from the bedroom of my youth.

3 medium to large yellow beets, tops cut off

1 tablespoon candied ginger

2 cups all-purpose flour

1 teaspoon salt

1 ½ teaspoons baking soda

½ teaspoon ground cardamom or cinnamon

¾ cup granulated sugar

¾ cup packed light brown sugar

6 tablespoons butter, melted

3 large eggs

1 teaspoon vanilla paste

Gold dusting powder (see Note)

12 edible paper gold crowns (see Note)

❶ Put the beets in a medium saucepan and cover with cold water. Place over medium-low heat and bring to a simmer. Cook for 20 to 30 minutes, or until the beets are fork tender. Remove from the heat and drain. When the beets are cool enough to handle, cut off the ends, peel, and chop. Set aside.

❷ In the bowl of a food processor, pulse the candied ginger until pulverized. Add the chopped beets and pulse until smooth (you should have 1 ½ to 1 ¾ cups beet puree). Set aside.

❸ Preheat the oven to 350° F. Line a 12-cup muffin tin with gold foil cupcake liners and set aside.

❹ In a medium mixing bowl, whisk together the flour, salt, baking soda, and cardamom. Set aside.

❺ In the bowl of a standing mixer fitted with the whisk attachment, cream together both sugars and the butter until light and fluffy. Add the eggs one at a time, and whisk until each addition is just incorporated. Add the vanilla paste and beet puree and whisk until thoroughly combined. With the mixer on low speed, gradually add the flour mixture and whisk until smooth.

❻ Fill the cupcake liners three-quarters full and bake for 22 to 25 minutes, until a toothpick inserted in the center of one cupcake comes out clean. Allow the cupcakes to cool in the pan completely before you remove and decorate them.

❼ Decorate each cupcake by brushing with a thin layer of gold dust powder and topping each with an edible gold paper crown, if desired . . . I have always desired a crown. ✳

*Gold dusting powder can be found at most craft stores in the baking section. The edible paper gold crowns can be found online, see Credits (page 213).*

# Hog Heaven Chocolate Cake

## (decadent chocolate cake topped with bacon + pecans)

### serves 24

Many years ago, on a pig farm in rural Missouri, I stuck my chocolate-covered palm into the pocket of my shorts and found a piece of bacon.

On summer days, one wasn't allowed in the farmhouse until mealtime. Grandma had a rusted hook-and-eye closure on the back screen door. The hook was always in the eye, locked from the inside. Thirsty? Grandma pointed to the garden hose. Bathroom break? Grandma pointed to the woods. Hungry? If you knew what was good for you, you wouldn't ask.

Grandma's meal schedule was never regular, either. Lunch may be at noon one day and at three P.M. the next. Grandchildren were not a priority, hypoglycemia be damned. It didn't take me long to learn to squirrel away food whenever Grandma laid the table for us to eat. After most breakfasts, I'd grab an extra piece of bacon and put it in my pocket on the chance she had better things to do come lunchtime.

One such day, I grabbed for my salty snack with a palm thoroughly coated with a melted chocolate bar. It was a grand revelation—four summers before Nixon's resignation—that changed my world and my palate forever.

That same summer, the sweet-and-salty, chocolate-and-bacon discovery won me a third-place ribbon at the county Youth Fair (there was no fourth place, but I didn't care) for my bacon chocolate cake. Clearly, as indicated by the judges, it wouldn't be until many years later that everyone else's palates would catch up to mine.

¾ cup dark unsweetened cocoa powder, sifted

½ cup very hot (almost boiling) strong coffee

3 cups sifted cake flour

1 teaspoon baking soda

½ teaspoon salt

1 ½ cups (3 sticks) butter, at room temperature

1 ¾ cups vanilla sugar (page 202) or regular sugar

4 large eggs

1 teaspoon vanilla paste

1 cup chocolate milk

1 ½ cups pecan halves, toasted

4 slices bacon, cooked extra crisp

2 recipes Rich Chocolate Buttercream Frosting (page 206)

❶ Preheat the oven to 350° F. Spray three 8-inch round cake pans with nonstick cooking spray, line the bottoms with parchment paper, and spray the paper. Set aside.

❷ In a medium mixing bowl, whisk together the cocoa powder and coffee and set aside to cool.

❸ In a separate medium mixing bowl, sift together the cake flour, baking soda, and salt and set aside.

❹ In the bowl of a standing mixer fitted with the paddle attachment, beat the butter until smooth. Gradually add the vanilla sugar and beat for 4 minutes, or until light and fluffy. Scrape down the bowl as needed. Add the eggs one at a time, beating well after each addition and scraping down the bowl as needed. Add the vanilla paste and beat just until combined.

⑤ Whisk the chocolate milk into the cooled cocoa-coffee mixture.

⑥ With the mixer on low speed, alternately add the flour and chocolate milk mixtures to the batter, starting and ending with the flour mixture. Mix for 3 minutes, or until the batter is smooth and creamy. Divide the batter evenly among the prepared pans. Bake for 30 minutes, rotating the pans halfway through for even baking, until a toothpick inserted in the center comes out clean. Let the layers cool in the pans for 20 minutes before turning out onto a cooling rack and removing the parchment paper.

⑦ Put the pecans and bacon in the bowl of a food processor and pulse a few times, until they are broken up, but not too fine, kind of a chunky pig fairy dust. Set aside.

⑧ Frost the cake (see "How to Frost a Layer Cake," page 16), using 1 heaping cup frosting for each layer and a crumb coat, then about 3 cups frosting for the final coat. (I like to make a smooth surface all over the cake and then use a piping bag fitted with a star tip to pipe around the entire edge of the cake top. This gives the cake a rimmed edge, so the pecans and bacon will stay in place). Sprinkle the top of the cake with the pecan and bacon mixture. ✳

# Bridge & Tunnel Cheesecake

## (hot caramel nut cheesecake)

### serves 16

It occurred to me that in creating this unique New York–style cheesecake, I had encompassed the stereotypical characteristics of my favorite boroughs of New York City—Brooklyn and Manhattan—into the recipe.

Brooklyn: The sweet and vicious spiced nuts make me think of this trendy borough. The addition of nuts to the cheesecake recipe practically screams to be recognized as the most important ingredient to the overall flavor. A hipster ingredient, if you will.

Manhattan: No surprise here! This recipe is defined by the showy, rich caramel sauce that wouldn't think about living anywhere else than on top of this cheesecake.

### For the cheesecake:

1 cup graham cracker crumbs

1 recipe Sweet and Vicious Nuts (recipe follows)

5 tablespoons butter

7 (8-ounce) packages cream cheese, at room temperature

1 cup granulated sugar

1 tablespoon vanilla paste

4 large eggs, at room temperature

½ cup sour cream

### For the caramel sauce:

½ cup (1 stick butter)

1¼ cups packed dark brown sugar

½ cup heavy cream

❶ Preheat the oven to 300° F. Spray a 9-inch springform pan with nonstick cooking spray, wrap the outside of the pan tightly with foil (this will help prevent any water from seeping in during baking), and set aside. Have a roasting pan that is wider and deeper than the springform pan ready and put a kettle of water on to boil.

❷ In the bowl of a food processor with the metal blade, combine the graham cracker crumbs, ½ cup nuts, and 5 tablespoons butter. Pulse until the mixture is finely ground. Use a spatula to press the mixture into the bottom and partially up the sides of the prepared springform pan. Set the pan in the center of the roasting pan.

❸ In the bowl of a standing mixer fitted with the paddle attachment, beat the cream cheese, granulated sugar, and vanilla paste until just smooth. You don't want a lot of air in your cheesecake batter, so don't overbeat. Add the eggs one at a time, beating until each addition is just incorporated. Scrape down the bowl as needed. Remove the bowl from the stand and fold in the sour cream until just incorporated.

❹ Pour the batter into the prepared springform pan sitting in the roasting pan and place in the oven. Pour hot water from the kettle into the roasting pan until it comes 1½ inches up the side of the springform pan. Bake for 2 to 2¼ hours, until the top is a honey golden brown and the cake is still a little wobbly in the center. Carefully remove the springform pan from the roasting pan and transfer to a cooling rack. Run a knife around the sides of the pan to loosen the cake and let it cool to room temperature. Before removing the cake from the pan, cover with plastic wrap and refrigerate overnight.

❺ **Make the caramel sauce:** In a medium saucepan over medium heat, whisk together the butter and the brown sugar until the butter has melted. Whisk in the cream and continue to stir for 5 minutes, until the sugar is dissolved and the mixture is smooth and creamy. Allow the sauce to cool completely before spreading it on the cheesecake.

⑥ To serve, spread a thin layer of the sauce over the top of the cheesecake. Top with the remaining nuts and drizzle with the remaining sauce. ✳

## Sweet and Vicious Nuts, yields 2 ½ cups

1 cup raw unsalted almonds, roughly chopped

1 cup unsalted cashews, roughly chopped

½ cup pecan halves, roughly chopped

2 large egg whites, lightly frothed using a fork

¼ cup packed light brown sugar

1 teaspoon ground chipotle

¼ teaspoon salt

**To make the Sweet & Vicious Nuts:**

❶ Preheat the oven to 325° F. Line a baking sheet with foil and set aside.

❷ In a medium mixing bowl, stir all the ingredients together until the nuts are well coated. Pour the mixture onto the prepared baking sheet and spread out in an even layer. Bake for 20 minutes, stirring often, until the nuts are golden brown. Let cool completely before using. ✳

✳

# Stoned & Grilled Cornmeal Cake

### (olive oil, stone fruit, + ground yellow corn)

#### serves 12

Olive oil in a cake? Yes! But won't my cake taste like a jar of olives? *No!* If this is your first try at using olive oil in a cake I know it won't be your last. Since olive oil contains natural emulsifiers, it helps ensure a richer, moister cake with a tender crumb. In this recipe, you'll notice I call for just "olive oil." Less expensive than extra-virgin, pure olive oil has a milder flavor and I find it best for baking.

3 to 4 large stone fruits (peaches or nectarines), or up to 6 smaller ones (apricots or plums), halved and pitted

6 tablespoons olive oil, plus more for grilling the fruit

1 ½ cups all-purpose flour

½ cup yellow cornmeal

2 teaspoons baking powder

½ teaspoon salt

2 large eggs

¾ cup vanilla sugar (page 202)

¼ teaspoon S&V House Blend Almond Extract (page 199) or regular almond extract (page 198)

1 cup milk

Cinnamon Whipped Cream (recipe follows)

❶ Heat a grill pan or outdoor grill to medium-high. Brush the fruit halves lightly with oil and place them cut side down on the hot grill. Grill for 3 minutes, or just until black marks form on the fruit. Transfer to a plate and set aside while you prepare the cake.

❷ Preheat the oven to 350° F. Butter a 9-inch round springform pan and set aside.

❸ In a medium bowl, whisk together the flour, cornmeal, baking powder, and salt. Set aside.

❹ In a large bowl, whisk together the oil, eggs, vanilla sugar, S&V House Blend almond extract, and milk until smooth. Stir in the flour mixture until just combined. The batter may be lumpy; don't sweat it. Pour the batter into the prepared pan and use a spatula to spread it evenly. Arrange the fruit cut side up on top of the batter. Bake for 30 to 35 minutes, until a toothpick inserted into the center of the cake comes out clean and the top of the cake springs back when lightly pressed. Let cool in the pan for at least 1 hour before removing the pan sides and slicing the cake. Serve with the whipped cream on the side. ✳

## Cinnamon Whipped Cream, yields about 2 cups

1 cup very cold heavy cream

3 tablespoons confectioners' sugar, sifted

¼ teaspoon ground cinnamon

Put the bowl and whisk attachment of a standing mixer in the freezer for 15 minutes (or use a deep metal bowl and a whisk). Fit the cold bowl and whisk attachment on the standing mixer, pour in the cream, and whisk until soft peaks form. Sprinkle with the confectioners' sugar and cinnamon and whisk until slightly stiffer peaks form. Be careful not to overbeat. ✳

I baked two of these cakes for the first time on the island of Sardinia, to the applause of 22 gorgeous sailors. It ranks as one of the greatest nights of my life.

The cake?
It was really good, too.

✳

# Lemonhead Cake

### (sweet + sour lemon cake)

**serves 20**

I love all sweet-and-sour foods: a half-ripe persimmon, cheap Chinese takeout, and Lemonhead candies. For a candy, Lemonheads have it all going on—a 1980's fashion-forward color, eye-squintingly sour outer shell, and a sweet, smooth center. It could possibly be the perfect candy, so I let it be the inspiration for this sweet and sour cake: tangy lemon layers with sweet, buttery frosting decorated with the candy it's named after. Finally! A sweet-and-sour dish that delivers and doesn't involve a sauce packet you have to open with your teeth.

2 ¾ cups cake flour

1 ⅔ cups sugar

1 tablespoon baking powder

¾ teaspoon salt

1 tablespoon grated lemon zest

¾ cup (1 ½ sticks) butter, at room temperature

4 large egg whites, plus 1 whole large egg

1 cup unsweetened coconut milk or regular whole milk

½ teaspoon lemon extract (page 199)

½ teaspoon vanilla paste

¼ cup Lemonhead syrup
(5 Lemonhead candies melted in ¼ cup water and cooled)

Swiss Meringue Buttercream Frosting (page 205),
tinted bright yellow with food coloring

2 (7-ounce) bags Lemonhead candies for garnish

❶ Preheat the oven to 350° F. Spray two 8-inch round cake pans with nonstick cooking spray, line the bottoms with parchment paper, and spray the paper. Set aside.

❷ In the bowl of a standing mixer fitted with the paddle attachment, combine the flour, sugar, baking powder, salt, and lemon zest and mix on low speed for 1 minute, or until just combined. Add the butter and increase the speed to medium. Mix for 2 to 3 minutes, until the mixture is a paste. Add the egg whites one at a time, beating well after each addition. Add the whole egg and beat to combine. Scrape down the bowl as needed. The batter will be thick.

❸ In a liquid measuring cup, stir together the coconut milk, lemon extract, and vanilla paste. With the mixer on medium speed, slowly pour this mixture into the batter. Beat for 3 to 5 minutes, until fluffy. Scrape down the bowl as needed. Divide the batter between the prepared pans and bake for 25 to 35 minutes, until a toothpick inserted in the center of the cake comes out clean. Let the cakes cool in the pans on a rack, then turn them out of the pans.

❹ Slice a thin layer of cake from the top of each layer to create a flat surface (save the trimmings for Cake Scrap Cookies, page 168). Place one layer (cut side up) on a cake pedestal or plate. Using a chopstick or skewer, poke a few holes in the top of the cake. Brush the top of the cake with half of the lemonhead syrup. Let the syrup seep into the holes. Spread 1 heaping cup frosting over the top of the first cake layer. Place the second cake layer on top of the frosting, cut side up, poke holes in the top, and brush the top with the remaining syrup. Spread 1 heaping cup frosting as a crumb layer (see "How to Frost a Layer Cake," page 16) to cover the entire cake (it's okay if you can see the cake through the frosting). Refrigerate for 30 minutes.

❺ Use the remaining frosting (about 3 cups) to apply the final decorative layer over the entire cake. Garnish with Lemonhead candies. (I love polka dots, so I piped dots all over the cake and then put a Lemonhead candy on each dot. You could cover the entire cake in Lemonheads, which would be unreal!) ✳

\*

# Spice Channel Cake

### (sexy spice cake, creamy mascarpone frosting)

serves 20

This cake has more spice than a Moroccan souk vendor. A heady blend of spices get the senses flowing, while the creamy mascarpone frosting cools everything down.

1 tablespoon ground cinnamon

1 teaspoon ground cardamom

½ teaspoon ground allspice

¼ teaspoon ground cloves

¼ teaspoon freshly grated nutmeg

1 teaspoon ground ginger

¼ teaspoon freshly ground black pepper

2 ¼ cups all-purpose flour

½ teaspoon baking powder

½ teaspoon baking soda

½ teaspoon salt

2 large whole eggs, plus 3 large egg yolks, at room temperature

½ teaspoon vanilla paste

1 cup (2 sticks) butter, at room temperature

1 ¾ cups vanilla sugar (page 202) or regular sugar

2 tablespoons molasses

1 cup buttermilk, at room temperature

Mascarpone Frosting (page 209)

❶ Preheat the oven to 350° F. Spray two 8-inch square baking pans with nonstick cooking spray, line the bottoms with parchment paper, and spray the paper. Set aside.

❷ In a small mixing bowl, whisk together the cinnamon, cardamom, allspice, cloves, nutmeg, ginger, and pepper. Reserve 1 teaspoon for use in the frosting.

❸ In a medium mixing bowl, whisk together the flour, baking powder, baking soda, salt, and spice mixture. Set aside.

❹ In a small mixing bowl, whisk together the eggs, egg yolks, and vanilla paste and set aside.

❺ In the bowl of a standing mixer fitted with the paddle attachment, cream the butter, vanilla sugar, and molasses together on medium-high speed for 4 minutes, or until light and fluffy. Scrape down the bowl as needed. Reduce the mixer speed to medium, add half of the egg mixture, and beat for 20 seconds, or until incorporated. Add the remaining egg mixture and beat again. Scrape down the bowl as needed. Reduce the speed to low and add about one-third of the flour mixture, followed by half of the buttermilk. After each addition, mix until just incorporated. Repeat the process, adding half of the remaining flour mixture and all the remaining buttermilk. Add the remaining flour mixture. Increase the speed to medium and mix for 20 seconds, or until thoroughly combined.

❻ Divide the batter evenly between the prepared pans. Bake for 30 minutes, or until the cake is just beginning to pull away from the sides of the pan and a toothpick inserted in the center comes out clean. Let the cakes cool completely in the pans, then turn them out of the pans.

❼ Stir the reserved spice mixture into the frosting. Frost the cake (see "How to Frost a Layer Cake," page 16), using 1 heaping cup frosting for each layer and the crumb coat, then about 2 cups frosting for the final decorative coat (I like to let the final frosting coat on this cake be a little messy . . . sexier . . . more fun). \*

✳

# Virgin Cake

## (Scandinavian almond cake)

serves 18

The first ten years of my son's life were spent in a world-class ski resort in Colorado. Two of those years were spent under the watchful eye of Sophie, his babysitter. Young girls from around the world would chase the snow and the lifestyle it brought to our town. They needed three things: a place to live, a job, and a ski pass. We provided Sophie with all three.

Sophie was an eighteen-year-old blond-haired beauty from Sweden with a shy personality and a penchant for baking. She taught me how to make a version of this delicious and light Scandinavian almond cake during our first Christmas together. By the time our second Christmas rolled around, the cake was the only thing that hadn't changed about Sophie.

Sophie arrived in our town a virgin. She did not leave the same.

## (Warning: Gluten Free)

### *Make Your Own Almond Flour*

*Roughly chop 3 cups raw whole almonds and put them in a food processor. Pulse just until the almond flour/meal is formed. If you mix too long, you'll end up with almond butter. Sift the almond flour to remove any bigger chunks before using. Note: If you live in a moist (I dislike that word almost as much as the word "popular") climate, toast your almonds in the oven to remove the moisture and let them cool before processing.*

*Most confectioners' sugars are gluten free, but be sure to check the label.*

¼ cup coconut oil, at room temperature, plus more for the pan

1 cup sugar

2 cups firmly packed almond flour, preferably homemade (see below left)

1 teaspoon baking powder

¼ teaspoon salt

4 tablespoons (½ stick) butter, at room temperature

3 large eggs

Grated zest and juice of 1 small orange

¼ cup unsweetened coconut milk

2 teaspoons almond extract (page 199)

Confectioners' sugar, for dusting (see Note)

❶ Preheat the oven to 350° F. Grease an almond cake pan (a 12-by-4 ½-inch loaf pan with a rounded and ridged bottom) with coconut oil. (Or use a 9-inch springform pan if you'd like, though it's not as pretty.) Set aside.

❷ In a medium mixing bowl, whisk together the sugar, almond flour, baking powder, and salt. Set aside.

❸ In the bowl of a standing mixer fitted with the whisk attachment, whisk the coconut oil and butter until just creamy. Add the eggs, orange zest, orange juice, and coconut milk and whisk until fully combined.

❹ With the mixer on low speed, gradually add the almond flour mixture, then add the almond extract and mix until incorporated.

❺ Pour the batter into the prepared pan and bake for 30 minutes. Cover the pan loosely with foil and continue to bake for 25 minutes, or until a toothpick inserted in the center comes out clean. Let cool in the pan completely, then remove the cake from the pan. Sprinkle with confectioners' sugar, slice, and serve. ✳

✳

# Chocolate Mug Cakes

## (orange slice candies baked inside a chocolate cake-filled mug)

### yields 4 cakes

My dad is a tall man with a big sweet tooth. His height has helped him in many ways: in college basketball, knocking the snow off the top of his car, intimidating underlings, and reaching for a faded white candy bowl he keeps on the highest kitchen shelf.

If you're a guest in my dad's home (and if he likes you), he'll make a production out of getting down the bowl of candy. His histrionics include fishing through its contents until he hands you that "special" piece he just knew you would love. It doesn't take a regular visitor much time to recognize the "special" pieces of candy he fishes out are not really special at all. In fact, my dad typically does a quick triage of the bowl before handing out his least favorite, but he does it all with great sales appeal.

It's only family insiders who know that ever since the big white candy bowl was new, there has also existed a smaller mug my father keeps in the shadows. Its contents are never offered up, neither to visitors nor to family. The contents of the small candy-filled mug that only a tall man can see? Chocolate bars and orange slices—my father's favorite. This treat is inspired by that top-shelf mug and its contents, a decadent chocolate cake studded with old-school orange slice candies baked inside a dad-sized mug.

½ cup (1 stick) butter, plus extra for the mugs

½ cup sugar, plus extra for the mugs

10 ounces bittersweet chocolate, coarsely chopped

4 large whole eggs

1 large egg yolk

½ teaspoon orange extract (page 199)

¼ teaspoon salt

¼ cup all-purpose flour

½ cup candied orange slices, chopped, plus more for decorating

A few drops of corn syrup, for decorating

1 tablespoon unsweetened cocoa powder, for decorating

❶ Preheat the oven to 375° F. Generously butter the insides of four 9-ounce oven-safe mugs (they should be stamped "oven-safe" on the bottom of the mug, but if in doubt, contact the manufacturer to be sure) and dust with sugar. Place on a baking sheet and set aside.

❷ Place a heatproof bowl over a saucepan of simmering water and put the chocolate and butter in the bowl. Heat, stirring often, until the chocolate is melted. Remove the bowl from the heat and let cool slightly.

❸ In a large mixing bowl, using a handheld mixer, beat the eggs, egg yolk, orange extract, salt, and sugar for 4 to 6 minutes, until the mixture is thick and foamy. Fold the flour into the chocolate mixture. With the mixer on low speed, gradually add the chocolate mixture to the egg mixture, beating until well combined. Fold in the candied orange pieces.

❹ Spoon the batter into the prepared mugs, filling them to within ½ inch of the top. Bake for 15 to 18 minutes, until the cakes begin to puff above the top of the mugs. Let cool for 15 minutes (the cakes will still be warm).

❺ **While the cakes are cooling, make the candy flower garnish:** Cut 4 pieces of candy into 4 lengthwise strips each (for a total of 16 pieces). Work each slice into a cone shape with your fingers (just have fun, no one is judging . . . except me). Use a dot of corn syrup to connect the thin ends of 4 cones to create a flower (you may need to pinch the ends together a bit). Repeat with the remaining pieces.

❻ Dust each mug cake with cocoa powder and top with an orange slice flower. Add a scoop of ice cream if you like. Serve while still warm, giving each guest a spoon. ✳

*

# Sunday Morning Panettone Muffins

## (sweet fruit bread muffins)

### yields 12

My family loves a big farm breakfast on Sunday mornings. It's our treat for eating well the rest of the week. There's always thick-cut bacon, some sort of eggs, and freshly baked bread. We are especially fond of panettone. Since I believe Sunday mornings are supposed to be easy (cue the Commodores here) on the eaters and the cooks, I started making this simpler version of panettone, using mini panettone paper baking molds. The texture is a bit different, but the taste and the thrill it gives my family are the same.

Would it be weird if I asked Lionel Richie to join us for breakfast one Sunday?

½ cup golden raisins

½ cup dried mango, diced

½ cup dried cherries, diced

¼ cup candied ginger, diced

¼ cup orange juice

2 tablespoons Gosling's Black Seal rum

4 tablespoons (½ stick) butter

2 tablespoons vegetable oil

⅔ cup vanilla sugar (page 202) or regular sugar

2 large eggs, at room temperature

¼ teaspoon S&V House Blend Citrus Extract (page 199)

½ teaspoon vanilla paste

2 ¼ cups all-purpose flour

2 teaspoons baking powder

½ teaspoon salt

⅔ cup milk

4 tablespoons turbinado sugar

❶ In a medium bowl, combine the raisins, mango, cherries, and ginger with the orange juice and rum. Cover and refrigerate overnight. (If you forget to soak your dried fruit overnight, place the fruit in a microwave-safe bowl with the liquid and microwave on high for 30 seconds. Let the fruit stand for 2 minutes before using.)

❷ Preheat the oven to 375° F. Place twelve 2 ½-by-1¾-inch) self-standing mini panettone paper baking molds on a baking sheet and set aside. If you do not have panettone baking molds, you can use a large muffin tin with paper liners, or just spray a large muffin tin with nonstick baking spray.

❸ In the bowl of a standing mixer fitted with the paddle attachment, cream together the butter, oil, and vanilla sugar until smooth. Add the eggs one at a time, beating well after each addition. Scrape down the bowl and reduce the mixer speed to low. Add the citrus extract and vanilla paste and stir until just combined.

❹ In a medium mixing bowl, whisk together the flour, baking powder, and salt. With the standing mixer on low, alternately add the flour mixture and the milk to the butter mixture, beginning and ending with the flour. Make sure everything is thoroughly combined and scrape down the bowl as needed. Use a spoon to stir in the fruit, along with any soaking liquid.

❺ Spoon the batter into the molds, filling them three-quarters full. Sprinkle the top of each muffin with 1 teaspoon of the turbinado sugar. Bake for 20 minutes, or until the tops of the muffins are a golden brown and a toothpick inserted in the center of one comes out clean. Remove from the oven and let the muffins cool enough to handle before you transfer them to a cooling rack to cool completely. *

\*

# The. Best. Ever. Red. Velvet. Cake.

## (less sugar, more flavor)

serves 12 to 16

"So what cake do you eat on your birthday?"
I asked the dreamy, blue-eyed sailor boy I had fallen for.
When he said red velvet cake, my heart sank.
I'd never heard of such a thing.

I made that first red velvet cake twenty-one years ago for
that boy, and a year later I married him. Now, between my
husband and my celebrity chef clients, I bake more red
velvet cakes than a Southern bakery on July 3rd. So, I set
out to perfect the recipe. And, finally, twenty-one years
to the day since he tasted my first red velvet cake, my
husband declared this recipe to be the best—ever.

My secret is using vanilla sugar in the cake—
far less than most recipes call for. I also use the best
cocoa powder and butter I can buy. The final stroke of
genius is the frosting: more tang and less sweet. You
have to trust me that this is the best red velvet cake
you will ever make; after all, I'm still married.

1 cup (2 sticks) organic butter

1 ½ cups vanilla sugar (page 202)

2 large farm-fresh eggs, at room temperature

2 tablespoons good-quality cocoa powder

2 ounces red liquid food coloring, plus more for decorating

2 ½ cups cake flour

1 teaspoon salt

1 cup buttermilk

½ teaspoon vanilla paste

½ teaspoon baking soda

1 tablespoon vinegar

Cream Cheese Frosting (page 206)

❶ Preheat the oven to 350° F. Spray two 9-inch round cake pans with nonstick cooking spray, line the bottoms with parchment paper, and spray the paper. Set aside.

❷ In the bowl of a standing mixer with the paddle attachment, beat the butter and vanilla sugar until light and fluffy. Add the eggs one at a time, beating well after each addition.

❸ In a separate small bowl, mix the cocoa and food coloring together with a fork; add to the butter mixture and mix well.

❹ Sift together the flour and salt and beat into the butter mixture in increments, alternating with the buttermilk, beginning and ending with the flour mixture. Scrape down the bowl as needed. Stir in the vanilla paste.

❺ In a small bowl, combine the baking soda and vinegar and stir this into the batter until just incorporated. Divide the batter evenly between the prepared pans. Bake for 20 minutes, or until a toothpick inserted in the center of the cakes comes out clean. Be sure not to overbake! Let cool in the pans completely, then remove from the pans.

❻ Frost the cake (see "How to Frost a Layer Cake," page 16), using 1 heaping cup frosting for the first layer, 2 heaping cups frosting as a crumb layer, and about 3 cups frosting for the final decorative coat. For a fun garnish, I like to dip the tip of a small offset spatula into ½ teaspoon red food coloring and drag the flat side along the sides of the frosted cake. It's a simple technique that makes a sweet cake look vicious. \*

# 2

# sweet breads & pastries

Salvation Cinnamon Rolls | Fruit Cobbler Bread

Chocolate Maniac Fire Bread | Hot Spiced Donut Holes | Chewy Chocolate Bread

Brioche | Eyes Wide Shut Bread | Puff Pastry | Sweet & Salty Palmiers | Cow Horns

*I keep my sweet breads and pastries—after they are completely cooled—at room temperature in airtight containers or wrapped tightly in plastic wrap. This will keep them fresh for up to 3 days. If you wrap them tightly and store them in the refrigerator they will keep for up to a week. For the best flavor and consistency, allow time for them to come to room temperature before eating. My family? They are much too impatient to wait for a baked treat to reach room temperature, so I keep everything in plain sight so it all gets eaten quickly.*

Opposite: Chewy Chocolate Bread, page 72

⁂

# Salvation Cinnamon Rolls

### (spicy decadent rolls, caramel cream cheese frosting)

yields 12 large rolls

When I moved to a rural coastal town in North Carolina as a young adult, I thought the town's eight churches were quaint, actually a selling point for the community. There was one church for every thirty-six residents—God was clearly present there. My yard was just steps away from the Methodist church and the Methodist church just steps away from my garden.

When you live in the South, there are long stretches in the middle of the year when the only time you can work in your garden is in the morning before the sun gets too hot (right around the time for early-morning Sunday church service). As folks would arrive, I was oftentimes in my garden doing what I liked to think of as the Lord's work, working the land. Sadly, the church folk didn't seem to think the same way. Headphones on and knee-deep in cow manure, I'd wave and smile as the congregants entered the side door. Unfortunately, the congregation didn't always see fit to reciprocate my friendly gesture. It was nearly a year before my family was invited to come to an event at the Methodist church. I learned that they were looking for a new pastor and had planned a welcoming breakfast for an especially promising candidate before he took the pulpit that morning. God didn't make me stupid—I knew my family meant three more people to help fill the pews and impress the possible pastor. It was a door cracked open and I wasn't about to slam it shut.

"Yes, we would love to come. What can I bring?" I asked.

"Nothing. Just bring yourselves," said the lady from the pulpit committee.

Even though I was raised Baptist, I knew you didn't walk into a Methodist event empty-handed. I baked a big sheet tray of these sweet and spicy rolls along with a quart-size Mason jar full of caramel cream cheese frosting. At the time, I just called them cinnamon rolls. After the prospective pastor mentioned them from the pulpit, I called them Salvation Cinnamon Rolls.

## For the dough:

½ cup (1 stick) plus ¾ cup (1 ½ sticks) butter, at room temperature, plus more for greasing

1 cup warm milk

¼ cup warm water, or more if needed

1 teaspoon vanilla extract (page 198)

3 teaspoons instant active dry yeast

2 large eggs, at room temperature, beaten

½ teaspoon salt

½ cup sugar

5 cups bread flour, plus more for dusting

## For the hellfire filling:

1 cup firmly packed brown sugar

4 to 5 tablespoons ground cinnamon

1 teaspoon ground cayenne

Caramel Cream Cheese Frosting (page 206)

*To kick up the heat, add a pinch of ground cayenne to the finished frosting.*

**❶ Make the dough:** Butter the inside of a large mixing bowl and set aside.

**❷** In the bowl of a standing mixer fitted with the dough hook, combine the milk, water, vanilla, ½ cup butter, the yeast, eggs, salt, sugar, and flour and mix for 4 to 5 minutes, until a soft elastic dough forms. The dough should be slightly tacky to the touch. If the dough is too moist, add additional flour, 1 tablespoon at a time. If the dough is too dry, add warm water, 1 tablespoon at a time. Continue to mix the dough for 5 minutes, until it becomes smooth and elastic.

**❸** Place the dough in the prepared mixing bowl, turning once to ensure that both sides are buttered, and cover with plastic wrap. Allow the dough to rise in a warm place for 1 hour, or until it has doubled in size.

**❹** Butter a 9-by-13-inch baking pan and set aside.

**❺ Make the hellfire filling:** In a small mixing bowl, stir together the brown sugar, cinnamon, and cayenne and set aside.

**❻** On a lightly floured work surface, roll the dough out to a 16-by-24-inch rectangle. Use your hands to spread the remaining ¾ cup butter over the top of the dough, making sure to butter all the way to the edges. Sprinkle the filling evenly over the butter. Starting with a long side, roll the dough into a slightly loose, long log (rolling the dough too tightly will make the centers of the rolls pop up when baking). Pinch the seam to seal.

**❼** Using a serrated knife, cut the log into twelve equal-width rolls and place them on the prepared baking pan, spacing the rolls so they do not touch. (At this point you can cover the pan with plastic wrap and refrigerate it overnight. Allow about 1½ hours for the rolls to double in size once you remove them from the refrigerator.) Cover the pan and place it in a warm place for 1 hour, or until the rolls have doubled in size.

**❽** Preheat the oven to 350° F.

**❾** Bake the rolls for 15 to 20 minutes, until golden brown. Remove from the oven and allow to cool slightly before topping with the frosting. Serve warm. ✳

*Salvation Cinnamon Rolls freeze brilliantly. After you have cut the log into twelve equal rolls, lay them flat in a zip-top bag and freeze. Since I have a small family, I like to wrap them individually in plastic wrap before I put them in the zip-top bag so I can bake off just a few at a time.*

✽

# Fruit Cobbler Bread

### (1 quick bread batter, 5 variations)

yields 1 loaf

This quick bread batter recipe is my go-to LBD. No matter what the season, I can pull it out and use whatever accessories (fruit) I have on hand to make it awe-inspiring. I've provided five bread recipes below that use this same batter, each with its own special compound butter topping.

3 cups sliced fruit (fruit options on page 66; no need to slice berries)

½ cup (1 stick) butter, melted and cooled

3 large eggs

1 teaspoon S&V House Citrus Extract (page 169)

2 cups all-purpose flour

¾ cup granulated sugar

¼ cup packed light brown sugar

1 ½ teaspoons baking powder

¼ teaspoon baking soda

¼ teaspoon salt

1 teaspoon ground cinnamon

Spiced Topping (recipe on page 66)

Compound butter (optional; recipes on page 66)

❶ Preheat the oven to 350° F. Spray a 9-by-5-inch loaf pan with nonstick cooking spray. Line the pan with a strip of parchment paper the width of your pan and long enough to hang over both sides by a couple of inches if draped across the middle. (I like to do this because it helps to pick the bread up out of the pan without crushing it; plus I like the way it looks. I'm pretty sure liking the way it looks is more important in this case. The parchment gets all browned and beautiful.)

❷ Set aside 10 pieces of fruit for garnish. Using a food processor with the blade attachment or a blender, process the remaining pieces of fruit until almost pureed. This should yield 1 cup puree, or slightly more.

❸ In the bowl of a standing mixer fitted with the paddle attachment, beat the processed fruit with the butter, eggs, and citrus extract until well blended.

❹ In a medium mixing bowl, whisk together the flour, granulated and brown sugars, baking powder, baking soda, salt, and cinnamon. With the mixer on low speed, add the butter mixture and beat until well combined. Scrape down the bowl as needed.

❺ Pour the batter into the prepared pan. Arrange the reserved fruit pieces on top of the batter in a decorative pattern (this is where you get to have fun—I like to overlap them). Sprinkle with the Spiced Topping. Bake for 50 to 60 minutes, until the bread is golden brown and a toothpick inserted in the center comes out clean. Transfer the pan to a rack to cool for 15 minutes. To remove from the pan, grab each side of the parchment paper and lift. Let the bread cool completely before serving. Serve warm and naked (the bread), or with one of the compound butter suggestions on page 66. ✽

*Quick breads are a great place to try out different infused sugars because they are a sponge for flavor and spice. The infused sugars add another layer of subtle flavor. Peach Cobbler Bread is wonderful with clove sugar. Strawberry Cobbler Bread becomes something completely different when you use lavender sugar in place of the plain. You get the idea . . . embrace infused sugars. The learning curve with quick breads is not steep.*

*

## Fruit Cobbler Bread, continued

## Spiced Topping, yields about ½ cup

¼ cup pecans, toasted and chopped

¼ teaspoon ground cinnamon

Pinch of ground cayenne

Pinch of flaky salt (I use Maldon) or kosher salt

¼ cup all-purpose flour

2 tablespoons dark brown sugar

2 tablespoons butter, at room temperature

Put all the ingredients in a medium mixing bowl and mix together with your hands until it reaches the consistency of thick sand, with chunks of pecans.

## Strawberry Cobbler Bread

Use strawberries as the fruit in the recipe. Serve with Balsamic Strawberry Butter.

### ❶ Balsamic Butter, yields ¾ cup

½ cup (1 stick) butter, at room temperature

6 strawberries, mashed

1 teaspoon prepared balsamic glaze, or more to taste

Mix all the ingredients together until well combined.

## Peach Cobbler Bread

Use fresh peaches as the fruit in the recipe. You can use canned peaches if you must; just be sure to drain first. Frozen peaches may also be used; be sure to thaw before using. Drizzle the bread with 2 tablespoons Caramel Sauce (page 46; use store-bought if you have to) after it has cooled slightly. Serve with Amaretto Peach Butter.

### ❷ Amaretto Peach Butter, yields ¾ cup

½ cup (1 stick) good-quality butter, at room temperature

4 peach slices, mashed

1 tablespoon amaretto liqueur, or ¼ teaspoon almond extract (page 198)

Mix all the ingredients together until well combined.

## Sour Cherry Cobbler Bread

Use pitted sour cherries as the fruit in the recipe. Because the growing season for cherries is short, you may substitute canned sour or tart cherries. Make sure they are pitted and drained. Serve with Salty Chocolate Butter.

### ❸ Salty Chocolate Butter, yields ¾ cup

½ cup good-quality butter, at room temperature

¼ cup freshly grated good-quality bitter-sweet chocolate (use a Microplane to grate)

½ teaspoon flaky salt (I use Maldon, or substitute another sea salt)

Mix all ingredients together until well combined.

## Blackberry Cobbler Bread

Use fresh or frozen blackberries as the fruit in the recipe. Push the top layer of berries into the batter a bit before you sprinkle with the topping. Serve with Blackberry Lemon Thyme Butter.

### ❹ Blackberry Lemon Thyme Butter

½ cup (1 stick) butter, at room temperature

6 blackberries, mashed

½ teaspoon grated lemon zest

½ teaspoon fresh thyme leaves

Mix all the ingredients together until well combined.

## Apricot Cobbler Bread

Use apricots as the fruit in the recipe. You can use canned apricots if you must; just be sure to drain first. Frozen apricots may also be used; be sure to thaw before using. Serve with Orange Blueberry Butter.

### ❺ Orange Blueberry Butter

½ cup (1 stick) butter, at room temperature

¼ cup mashed blueberries

Juice and grated zest of ½ orange

Mix all the ingredients together until well combined.

✳

# Chocolate Maniac Fire Bread

## (spiced chocolate quick bread, smoked salty raspberry butter)

### yields 2 loaves

I'd rather watch a torturous loop of the movie *Flashdance* for three days than give you a quick bread recipe that is so 1980s . . . like banana bread. It doesn't matter if it's the best banana bread recipe ever—Blue Ribbon Banana Bread, Easy Banana Bread, Low-Fat Banana Bread, Grandma's Banana Bread, or my favorite title: Bangin' Banana Bread. Banana bread is banana bread. A monkey could make it, and it would still be darn good (btw: I love banana bread).

Instead, I am giving you a quick bread recipe that will set your mouth on fire with dark chocolate delight. Take off your leg warmers and give this bread a go.

1 ½ cups all-purpose flour

¼ cup unsweetened dark cocoa powder

½ teaspoon ground cinnamon

1 teaspoon salt

½ teaspoon baking soda

2 teaspoons baking powder

1 ½ cups packed light brown sugar

½ cup (1 stick) butter, melted and cooled to room temperature

2 large eggs, slightly beaten

1 cup applesauce

1 teaspoon vanilla paste

1 serrano chile, stemmed and minced (about 1 teaspoon)

¼ cup milk

1 cup roughly chopped dark chocolate (your favorite brand)

Raspberry Smoked Salty Butter (recipe follows)

❶ Preheat the oven to 350° F. Spray two 9-by 5-inch loaf pans with nonstick cooking spray. Line each pan with a strip of parchment paper the width of your pan and long enough to hang over both sides by a couple of inches if draped across the middle (this method gives you two handles to pull the finished bread out). Set aside.

❷ In a medium mixing bowl, whisk together the flour, cocoa powder, cinnamon, salt, baking soda, and baking powder.

❸ In a large mixing bowl, combine the brown sugar and butter and blend until just combined. Add the eggs, applesauce, vanilla paste, chile, and milk. Stir gently with a wooden spoon to combine. Stir in the flour mixture, mixing gently until combined. Fold in ½ cup of the chocolate pieces.

❹ Divide the batter between the prepared pans. Sprinkle the remaining ½ cup dark chocolate pieces down the center of each loaf lengthwise and pat them down into the batter to just below the surface. Bake for 50 minutes, or until a toothpick inserted in the middle of each loaf comes out clean. Let cool in the pan for a few minutes before turning out. To turn out, grab each side of the parchment paper and lift. Let cool completely before slicing and serve on its own or with the Raspberry Smoked Salty Butter. ✳

## Raspberry Smoked Salty Butter, yields ¾ cup

½ cup (1 stick) butter, at room temperature

¼ cup raspberries, mashed

⅛ teaspoon fine smoked salt
(I use alderwood smoked salt; a little goes a long way)

Mix all the ingredients together. ✳

\*

# Hot Spiced Donut Holes

## (small + spicy donut poppers)

### yields about 100 donuts

Donuts are the devil. They are the mischievous evil spirits of the diet world. If someone says they can make a low-fat donut that tastes good, they are lying to you. If you're okay with that (I am), then eat on. I try to trick myself into believing donuts are not so bad when you don't fry them and when the recipe doesn't have too much sugar and when they are small enough to pop in your mouth and when they contain red pepper, which has a myriad of health benefits. This logic works for me; it may be orchestrated by the devil, but the devil is a good cook, and I'm okay with that, too.

2 tablespoons plus 1 cup (2 sticks) butter, melted, plus more for greasing

1 ⅓ cups warm milk

2 teaspoons active dry yeast

⅓ cup plus 1 ½ cups granulated sugar

5 cups all-purpose flour, plus more for dusting

1 teaspoon salt

¼ teaspoon freshly grated nutmeg

2 large eggs

⅓ cup red pepper flake sugar (page 204)

1 tablespoon ground cinnamon

\*

❶ Grease a large mixing bowl with butter and set aside. In the bowl of a standing mixer, stir together the milk, yeast, ⅓ cup granulated sugar, and 2 tablespoons melted butter with a spoon. Let the mixture rest for about 5 minutes, until the yeast starts to foam.

❷ In a large mixing bowl, sift together the flour, salt, and nutmeg.

❸ Fit a dough hook on the standing mixer. With the mixer on low speed, add the eggs, red pepper flake sugar, and the flour mixture and beat for 3 minutes, until the dough is smooth and tacky and pulls away from the side of the bowl. At this point, you can adjust the dough's texture if needed. Add a little more milk if it is too dry, or a little more flour if it is too wet; the goal is for it to be smooth and tacky. Continue mixing the dough for 5 minutes more, until it becomes smooth and shiny. Transfer the dough to the prepared mixing bowl and turn over so both sides of the dough are buttered. Cover the bowl with plastic wrap and let the dough rise for about 1 hour, until it has doubled in size.

❹ Line two or three baking sheets with parchment paper and set aside. Punch the dough down and roll it out on a lightly floured surface to ½ inch thick. Using a donut-hole cutter or a small (1-inch) ring mold, cut out circles of dough and transfer them to the baking sheets, leaving about 1 inch between the circles. Cover the tray with lightly greased plastic wrap. (At this point, you can refrigerate the donuts overnight, then let them rise in the morning before baking.) Let the donuts rise for about 45 minutes, until they are puffed and nearly doubled.

❺ Preheat the oven to 375° F. In a medium mixing bowl, stir together the remaining 1½ cups granulated sugar and the cinnamon and set aside. Pour the remaining 1 cup butter into a separate bowl.

❻ Bake the donut holes for 5 to 7 minutes, until the bottoms of the donuts are just golden brown. The donuts should be pale on the top, and the insides just barely baked through. They will continue to bake after they are removed from the oven. Cool for 2 minutes, then dip them into the melted butter just to moisten and roll them in the cinnamon-sugar mixture to coat. Serve immediately.

✳

# Chewy Chocolate Bread
### (loads of chocolate but barely sweet)
#### yields 1 loaf

I live in a neighborhood of seventeen houses and twenty-two children (the odds are against me). I've tested this recipe on many of my adult neighbors and they love it, but it was the children who seemed extra-excited and intrigued by the large, round chocolate loaf. One curly-yellow-haired girl in particular would punch through the crust with her fingers when she thought no one was looking and scoop out a chunk of the soft chocolate center to eat. The young girl's name is Anne Chaddock, and she is a supergirl who runs the neighborhood fueled by my Chewy Chocolate Bread!

½ cup warm water

1 teaspoon active dry yeast

⅓ cup sugar

1 cup whole wheat flour

2 ⅓ cups all-purpose flour, plus more for dusting

⅓ cup good-quality unsweetened cocoa powder

1 ¼ teaspoons salt

Cornmeal, for dusting

½ cup good-quality dark chocolate, coarsely chopped

1 tablespoon turbinado sugar, for sprinkling

(Warning: this is kid friendly)

❶ In the bowl of a standing mixer fitted with the dough hook, combine the warm water, yeast, and 1 teaspoon of the sugar, mixing with your finger until the yeast is dissolved. Let the mixture rest for 10 minutes, until the yeast begins to foam. With the mixer on low speed, add 1¼ cups room-temperature water, the whole wheat flour, all-purpose flour, cocoa powder, and salt. Mix just until the dough is blended. Cover the bowl with plastic wrap and let rest at warm room temperature for 8 hours (I like to do this overnight).

❷ Line a baking sheet with a kitchen towel that has been dusted with cornmeal. Set aside.

❸ Turn the dough out onto a liberally floured work surface and pour the chocolate chunks over the top. Sprinkle with more flour before folding the dough over itself a few times to evenly distribute the chocolate. Shape the dough into a ball and transfer it, seam side down, to the prepared baking sheet. Dust the top of the dough ball with cornmeal, cover it with a kitchen towel, and let it rise about 2 hours, or until the dough has doubled in size.

❹ Preheat the oven to 450° F. Place a heavy cast-iron (or ceramic) 6- to 8-quart pot with a lid in the oven to heat until the oven comes to temperature.

❺ Carefully remove the heated pot from the oven and place the dough in it (seam side up or down—it doesn't matter). Don't worry if it looks like a hot mess; it will bake up beautifully. Brush the dough with water and sprinkle with the turbinado sugar. Cover the pot and return it to the oven to bake for 30 minutes. After 30 minutes, remove the lid and continue to bake for another 20 minutes, or until the loaf is a gorgeous dark brown and gives a dull sound when thumped. Let the bread cool before eating. ✳

See finished bread on page 57

# Brioche

### (tender sweet bread)

yields 1 loaf

Making brioche is for the bakers who possess attitude, swagger, and who consider themselves to be a bit Francophilic. The attitude and swagger helps them to caress the soft buttery dough into the perfect shape, while their Francophile side gives them enough courage to announce that "one doesn't cut brioche, one tears it. Cutting brioche is for the bourgeois."

I hope you love making brioche as much as I do.
*Vive la France!*

1 teaspoon active dry yeast

2 tablespoons milk, lukewarm

2 ½ cups all-purpose flour, plus more for dusting

1 teaspoon salt

5 large eggs, plus 2 large egg yolks, at room temperature

½ cup (1 stick) good-quality butter, at room temperature, plus more for buttering the pan

2 tablespoons superfine sugar (pulse granulated sugar in a food processor a couple of times)

½ teaspoon S&V House Citrus Extract (page 199)

1 tablespoon honey

Pinch of kosher or sea salt

*Brioche should be eaten the day it is made, preferably as soon as it has cooled. If you do have any leftovers, leave them out uncovered and use in the morning for French toast or the best "toad in the hole" known to man (or child).*

❶ In the bowl of a standing mixer fitted with the dough hook, combine the yeast and milk, stirring with your finger until the yeast is dissolved. Add the flour and salt and mix on low speed just until combined. Add 4 of the eggs and the 2 egg yolks, increase the mixer speed to medium, and beat for 2 minutes, or until the dough begins to come together. Scrape down the bowl as needed. Add the butter, superfine sugar, and citrus extract and beat for 5 minutes, until the dough starts pulling away from the side of the bowl and becomes glossy and elastic (the dough should be very soft, almost a batter).

❷ Cover the bowl with plastic wrap and let the dough rise in a warm place for 2 hours, until it has doubled in size (the dough will rise and then flatten on top a bit). Lift the dough out of the bowl, then let it fall back into the bowl to deflate. Cover and refrigerate overnight. Check the dough during the first few hours of chilling and repeat the process as needed to deflate the dough.

❸ Butter a 9-inch brioche mold or deep round cake pan. Set aside.

❹ In a small bowl, whisk together the remaining egg, the honey, and salt.

❺ Dust a work surface and your hands with flour. Divide the dough into three equal portions. Combine two portions and shape them into a ball. Place the ball in the brioche mold. Form the remaining portion into an egg shape. Using two fingers, punch a hole in the middle of the dough in the brioche mold and place the smaller egg-shaped portion of dough in the hole, making sure a bit of the dough sticks out the top. Brush the brioche dough with half of the egg-honey mixture, cover the mold with greased plastic wrap, and let the dough rise at room temperature for 1 to 2 hours, until it fills the pan.

❻ Preheat the oven to 400° F.

❼ Brush the top of the brioche dough again with the remaining egg-honey mixture. Bake for 30 to 40 minutes, until the brioche is a rich golden brown and the pan sounds hollow when tapped underneath. Let the brioche cool in the pan for 10 minutes before turning out onto a rack to cool completely. ✳

✳

# Eyes Wide Shut Bread

### (an apricot + rosemary chewy loaf)

#### yields 2 loaves

Sometimes you can see more clearly with your eyes closed. Eyes closed, a bite of a hot dog with the works and I'm an adolescent again, sitting on the bleachers at Wrigley Field. Close my eyes and a bite of a fried pork tenderloin sandwich takes me back to the warmth of my grandmother Lula Mae's kitchen. Sea urchin roe with a squeeze of lemon? I'm transported to a secluded beach in Greece and a vision of a boy who was never a gentleman.

When I close my eyes and take a bite of this apricot bread—with chunks of sweet apricots and hints of rosemary—I'm back on the island of Sardinia with the love of my life. If I open my eyes, I'm in my Savannah kitchen with the same man. I guess sometimes you don't need to bother closing your eyes when heaven is staring right at you . . . blue eyes shining, and a mouthful of apricot bread.

2 cups warm water

1 ½ teaspoons active dry yeast

2 teaspoons honey

1 tablespoon olive oil

2 ½ cups whole wheat flour

2 ½ cups bread flour, plus more for dusting

2 teaspoons salt

1 tablespoon chopped fresh rosemary

⅔ cup dried apricots, roughly chopped

1 tablespoon cornmeal

*Any apricots that are on the surface of the dough will turn dark when baking. This charred, sweet flavor is my favorite part of this bread.*

❶ In the bowl of a standing mixer fitted with the dough hook attachment, stir the water, yeast, honey, and oil with a spoon until the yeast dissolves. Let the mixture rest for 5 minutes, until the yeast begins to foam. Add both flours and the salt and mix until the dough is a messy, ugly ball. Let rest for 5 minutes.

❷ Add the rosemary and apricots and continue to mix for about 4 minutes, until the dough is firm and smooth and the rosemary and apricots are evenly distributed.

❸ Cover the bowl with a kitchen towel and let the dough rest for 1 hour. Line a baking sheet with parchment paper.

❹ Remove the dough from the bowl and turn out onto a lightly floured surface. Divide the dough into two equal portions and shape them into rounds. Place the rounds on the prepared baking sheet, cover with a kitchen towel, and let them rest for 1 to 1½ hours, until they have doubled in size. (I prefer to let the dough rise in proofing baskets, but if you don't have any don't worry, just use a parchment-lined baking sheet. If you do use baskets, dust them first with flour and shake out any excess flour, then place the rounds of dough, seam side up, in the basket. Cover with a kitchen towel and let them rise as directed.)

❺ Preheat the oven to 450° F. Place any size cast-iron skillet in the bottom of the oven, and a baking stone or baking sheet on the middle rack of the oven to preheat, too.

❻ Using a serrated knife or a razor blade, score the tops of the loaves, making an X that is ¼ inch deep (if using proofing baskets, turn the loaves over and gently remove from the baskets before scoring the top). Dust the baking stone or baking sheet with cornmeal and place the loaves, scored side up, on it. Add 1 cup ice cubes to the cast-iron skillet and close the oven door. Bake for 20 minutes, then lower the oven temperature to 425° F and continue to bake for 20 minutes more, until the loaves are a rich brown color. ✳

show & tell

# Puff Pastry

(flaky, buttery pastry so worth the effort) yields 2 pounds dough

2 cups (4 sticks) butter, at room temperature

3 ¼ cups all-purpose flour, plus more for dusting

1 ¼ cups very cold water

2 teaspoons salt

Juice of 1 lemon

Rewards can come in different forms.

When I was eight years old, I received a silver dollar from an elderly lady when my mother made me return the small crocheted coin purse the lady had dropped in front of me. Within the few short seconds before its return, I may have looked inside and counted four dollars and twenty-seven cents (counting money was always my best math skill).

Aside from that first 23 percent tip, making puff pastry is the best reward I've ever received. The reward was not only learning how to make a buttery, flaky pastry, it also came in the form of learning how important it is to spend time doing something right.

Making puff pastry takes me three hours, start to finish—the same time spent at a bad movie, on a bad date, or at a bad baby shower. Think about it. I'd much rather be biting into a crunchy palmier, wouldn't you?

*Puff pastry dough can be wrapped tightly in plastic wrap and refrigerated for 2 to 3 days or frozen for up to 1 month. If using frozen dough, thaw completely in the refrigerator before using.*

1. In the bowl of a standing mixer fitted with the paddle attachment, mix the butter and ½ cup of the flour. Mix for 2 minutes, or until the flour is fully incorporated into the butter and the mixture is nice and creamy.

2. Tear off a large piece of plastic wrap and place it on a cool work surface. Heap the butter mixture into the middle of the plastic wrap. Fold the plastic wrap over to cover and pat the butter into a 5-inch square. Wrap the butter block tightly and refrigerate until ready to use.

3. Working in a cool room, put the flour, cold water, salt, and lemon juice in the bowl of the standing mixer fitted with the dough hook. Mix just until a smooth, elastic dough is formed. If you need to add more water, add 1 tablespoon at a time and mix to combine. Turn the dough out onto a flour-dusted, cool work surface and shape into a ball. Brush off any excess flour and score the top of the ball with a sharp knife. Allow the dough to rest for 15 minutes before rolling it out to a rectangular shape about 6 by 12 inches, ¼ inch thick. Wrap in plastic wrap and refrigerate for 30 minutes.

4. Remove the butter block and the dough from the refrigerator and take off the plastic wrap. Working on a lightly floured surface, place the butter block in the middle of the chilled dough rectangle and wrap the sides of the dough over to completely cover the butter, pressing to seal.

*continued on page 78*

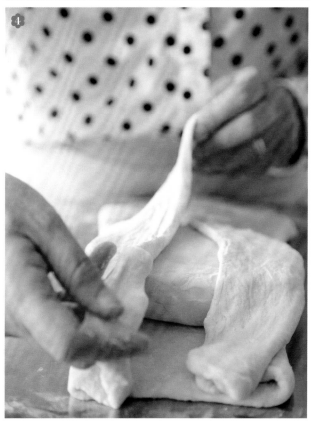

show & tell

## Puff Pastry, continued

**5** Gently roll the dough out to about a 9-by-20-inch rectangle, applying pressure evenly so the butter won't ooze out. Brush off any excess flour.

**6** Make a rectangular shape with three layers by folding both of the short ends in so they overlap in the center, as you would fold a letter to put into an envelope. Brush off any excess flour. Press your finger lightly into the top of the dough once (this will help you remember what fold you are on when this process is repeated). Wrap the dough in plastic wrap and refrigerate for another 15 minutes.

**7** Turn the cold dough out onto a lightly floured, cold work surface, and turn a quarter turn so the folds are going the opposite way as the last turn. Gently roll out again to about a 9-by-20-inch rectangle.

**8** Repeat the same letter-fold process, brush off any excess flour, and press your finger lightly into the top of the dough two times so you know this was rolled out twice. Wrap and refrigerate for 15 minutes.

**9** Repeat this process (called a turn) a total of six times, refrigerating after each turn. Once the dough has chilled after your last turn, the dough is ready to use.

*Never throw away your scraps! Like pie dough and cake scraps, I would never throw any puff pastry dough scraps away. Combine all the scraps and lightly knead them together. Roll out thinly. Cut into long thin strips, top with freshly grated cheese, and bake for quick cheese straws. Cut into small circles and bake off for the bases of appetizer bites; you can top them with anything. One of my favorite things to do is cut scraps into fun shapes with small cookie cutters and use them to garnish soups.*

*Why make just one? When I make puff pastry, I have two doughs working at once. The timing works out perfectly for me. By the time I do a turn on one dough, the other has been in the refrigerator for 15 minutes so it's a perfect rotation time. Doing two doughs always allows me to have an extra in the freezer.*

# Sweet & Salty Palmiers
## (crisp layered pastries)
### yields 36 (18 of each kind)

The first time I ate a palmier was in the Lesser Antilles on the French island of Martinique. The palmiers were stacked three-foot high at a roadside bakery. Each cookie was the size of my head (I'm told I have a big head), crisp, buttery, and sweet. The French locals would order one and share it among three. I ordered three and shared them with no one. Once I started making my own puff pastry, I would experiment with sweet and savory palmier fillings. I stuffed them with everything from sardines to homemade preserves and found out one very important thing. Palmiers are like baked potatoes—you can stuff them with just about anything and they taste great!

1 cup sugar

½ teaspoon cinnamon

⅛ teaspoon ground cayenne

All-purpose flour, for dusting

1 recipe Puff Pastry (page 76)

1 teaspoon coarsely ground black pepper

½ heaping cup chopped Kalamata olives

1 large egg, beaten with 1 tablespoon water

❶ Preheat the oven to 425° F. Line two baking sheets with parchment paper and set aside.

❷ In a small mixing bowl, stir together the sugar, cinnamon, and cayenne and set aside.

❸ On a lightly floured work surface, roll out the puff pastry dough to a rectangle, ¼ inch thick. Divide the dough in half (cutting through the width of the dough).

❹ Brush the top of each piece of dough with the egg wash. On one piece of dough, sprinkle the sugar mixture across the top, completely covering it to the edges. Press the sugar mixture gently into the dough. On the other piece of dough, sprinkle the pepper evenly across the top, then spread the chopped olives evenly over the pepper. Press the olives gently into the dough.

❺ Work with one piece of dough at a time to form the palmiers. Roll the longest side of the dough inward to form a long tube, until it just reaches the middle. Now, turn the dough around and roll the other side toward the middle until this tube touches the first (imagine the shape of an ancient scroll). Brush the seam where they meet with the egg wash. With a sharp knife, cut the rolled dough into ¾-inch-thick slices. Place the cut pieces flat side down on the prepared baking sheets, leaving 2 inches between them.

❻ Roll and cut the other piece of dough in the same manner. If you have room in your oven, bake both kinds of palmiers at once; if not, refrigerate one until ready to bake. Bake for 10 minutes, then carefully turn the palmiers over using a spatula (be careful: the good stuff oozing out will be very hot!). Continue to bake for another 10 minutes, until they are golden brown. Let cool before serving. ✳

# Sweet Breads & Pastries

*Palmiers are a perfect hostess gift. If you're anything like me, you're usually exhausted the morning after a party, not quite clear-headed and cleaning up a mess. I'm typically so busy managing the fallout from things that might have gotten a little out of hand that I don't have time for breakfast. Having a crunchy sweet palmier alongside an iced latte would be heaven.*

*My thoughts on store-bought frozen puff pastry? It's like a flu-shot: I don't think it works and I don't believe in it, but I get one every year anyway.*

✳

# Cow Horns

### (flaky puff pastry, citrus cream filling)

**yields 12**

As a little girl, it wasn't often I got to go on outings with just my dad. Typically, one of my older sisters horned in to ruin the fun, or, more often, my dad would escape by himself for what was, I imagine, a moment of quiet repose from a household filled with estrogen and acetone (I have two older sisters and no brothers).

A single-purpose store outing always required special clothes. I picked out my outfit carefully. A white sleeveless blouse embroidered overall with a small cherry print and coordinating red knit shorts. The red Keds I had hated when Mom brought them home two months prior were suddenly the perfect footgear. I was ready . . . if only my ears were pierced.

At the bakery, the weirdly sweet scents of frostings, fried donuts, and fritters all mixed together and lodged in the fibers of my cherry-stitched blouse. Dad ordered a white box full of pastries and told me I could choose one thing— anything—but I had to eat it before I got home.

The pastry decision didn't take long. I chose an apple fritter, not because I knew what an apple fritter tasted like, but because it was the biggest thing in the glass case. When I pointed to the fritter, my dad shook his head "no." He leaned down and whispered in my ear, "Fritters are for other people." I don't know who these other people were, but I imagined they were happy people with crystal-icing smiles.

In typical patriarchal form, Dad informed me that my favorite pastry must be a cow horn. He pointed into the case and told me to look at how the pastry was shaped like the cows' horns I'd seen on my grandparents' farm. "In France, they call them cream horns," he said.

I didn't know where this France was he was talking about, but I sure wasn't excited about eating something that came off a cow's head. Especially since I'd witnessed firsthand what came out the other end.

Dad ordered us both a cow horn from a salesgirl with chipped pink fingernail polish. I watched as my dad took the first bite before following suit. Even though the creamy center went halfway up my nose and the flaky outside shed pastry shards that landed on my red Keds, it was the best pastry I have ever put in my mouth. Not only because it tasted so good, but because I was eating it in a real bakery with just my dad. If only I had my ears pierced.

**For the horns:**

2 tablespoons butter, at room temperature

1 recipe Puff Pastry (page 76)

½ cup sugar

1 large egg yolk, beaten with 1 tablespoon water or milk

12 (5-inch-long) cream horn molds

**For the cream filling:**

2 cups cold heavy cream

¼ cup sifted confectioners' sugar

1 teaspoon S&V House Blend Citrus Extract (page 199)

❶ **Make the horns:** Grease twelve cream horn molds with the butter and set aside. Line a baking sheet with parchment paper and set aside. Have a small bowl of cold water ready.

❷ Roll the puff pastry out to a 12-inch square, about ¼ inch thick. Cut the dough into twelve 1-inch-wide strips. Work with one strip and one mold at a time. Brush the strip of dough lightly with the cold water. Starting at one end of the mold, roll the dough loosely around the mold, overlapping the dough slightly as you go. (An ever-so-slight gap between the pastry and the mold will allow you to remove the pastry from the mold more easily after it's baked.) Place the molds on the prepared baking sheet and repeat the process using the rest of the dough and molds. Refrigerate the horns for 30 minutes.

❸ Preheat the oven to 425° F. Pour the sugar onto a flat plate and set aside.

❹ Remove the chilled horns from the refrigerator and brush with the egg wash. Roll the horns in the sugar and return them to the baking sheet. Bake for 20 to 30 minutes, until the horns are golden brown. Remove from the oven and, when cool enough to handle, carefully remove the molds from the horns. Let the horns cool completely before filling.

❺ **Make the cream filling:** In the bowl of a standing mixer fitted with the whisk attachment, beat the cream on medium speed until it begins to thicken. Add the sugar and citrus extract and continue to beat until smooth and thick.

❻ Using a pastry bag and decorative tip (your call) or a long-handled spoon, fill the horns with the filling. Serve immediately. \*

*Cream horn molds are cylinder-shaped molds. They come in varying sizes and are most often used for shaping cannoli. If you don't have a mold, don't let it stop you. In a pinch, I've shaped tightly packed aluminum foil into 5-inch long cylinders about 1-inch in diameter (think of a hot dog shape) and it worked great!*

# savory breads

*My first rule of bread storage is to never put it in the refrigerator. Never. There's a lot of bread science behind this reasoning that involves starch molecules changing their alignment, which causes bread to go stale faster than it would if it were sitting on the counter. For loaves, I slice off just the amount I need from the loaf, then place it cut side down on a cutting board and cover it loosely with a kitchen towel. That's it. For bagels, crackers, flatbreads, naan, and biscuits, I seal them in a zip-top bag and store at room temperature. All will keep for up to 3 days.*

*When freezing any bread, make sure it is tightly wrapped in plastic so it can retain its moisture. When ready to eat, let the bread come to room temperature, then put it in a 350° F oven for 10 minutes. Breads will keep in the freezer for up to 3 months.*

*The baguette is an exception to this bread-storing rule. A baguette is meant to be eaten the day you make it. In France, it's considered a daily bread, and my French friends would never eat a day-old baguette unless they were gueule de bois (that's French for hungover).*

Opposite: Napoleon Bread, page 116

# 1 Potato 2 Potato 3 Potato Rolls

## (russet, sweet, + purple)

### yields 24 rolls

Potato rolls were the only rolls I remember my grandma Lula Mae baking. Baking requires two qualities Grandma didn't have: patience and precision. No one would argue that she could cook the hell out of a side of pork, but make a cake or bake bread? Let's just say flour was not her medium. As I remember, it was quite a production even when she was thickening gravy. When she finally did find the flour tin (it was not allowed to take up counter space), she would open the top and scrutinize the contents, pushing the flour from left to right with her abnormally long index finger. It wasn't until much later in my life that I realized she was looking for weevils.

Lula Mae had a big garden behind the barn where she planted, among other things, rows and rows of potatoes. The potato rows yielded enough each year to feed her large family and pack a Missouri root cellar so full that there would be no chance of our survival in the event of a tornado. Along with pork, there was a bowl of potatoes at every meal. Mostly boiled and buttered, or mashed. Sometimes fried. Never baked. Grandma had rules.

Leftover potatoes were never thrown away. They were placed in the "leftover potato bowl," a frog-green, oddly shaped Tupperware bowl with a lid that was supposed to make a burping sound when it was closed. It never did. As a kid, I saw Grandma transform the contents of the leftover potato bowl into everything from pancakes to dumplings, meat pie toppers, and my favorite: potato rolls. The one baked thing even Grandma couldn't screw up.

1 cup mashed russet potato, sweet potato, or purple potato (choose one)

2 tablespoons brown sugar

1 cup milk

3 to 4 cups bread flour

2 teaspoons salt

2 teaspoons instant yeast

Vegetable oil, for the bowl

1 egg, beaten with 1 tablespoon water

2 tablespoons poppy or sesame seeds (optional)

4 tablespoons butter

❶ Line a baking sheet with parchment paper and set aside.

❷ In the bowl of a standing mixer (removed from the mixer), combine the potato, brown sugar, and milk and stir to make a paste. Mix in 2 cups of the flour, the salt, and yeast (plus any spices you are using if using one of the variations listed below) and mix by hand until thoroughly combined (it's okay to have a few lumps of potato here). Place the mixing bowl on the standing mixer fitted with the dough hook and mix on low speed for about 5 minutes, adding ¼ cup flour at a time and mixing well after each addition until the dough is soft and tacky. Turn the dough out onto a lightly floured work surface and knead by hand for an additional 5 to 10 minutes, until the dough becomes firmer but is still soft and elastic.

❸ Shape the dough into a single ball and place in a lightly oiled bowl. Cover the bowl with plastic wrap and let rise at room temperature for 40 minutes to 1 hour, until the dough has doubled in size.

*continued on page 88*

❹ Turn the dough out onto a lightly floured work surface, divide into twenty-four equal pieces, and cover the pieces with plastic wrap. Working with one piece of dough at a time (keep the rest covered with plastic wrap), form it into a smooth, tight round. (To make a round dough ball, set the dough on a nonfloured work surface and grab loosely with your hand. With your fingers lightly wrapped around the dough, move your hand in small circular motions.)

❺ Arrange the dough balls on the prepared baking sheet with the sides of the rolls touching. Brush any extra flour off the rolls and cover loosely with plastic wrap. Let rise at room temperature for 40 minutes, or until the rolls have doubled in size.

❻ Preheat the oven to 375° F. Place a rack in the middle of the oven.

❼ Brush the rolls with the egg wash and sprinkle them with the seeds if you like. Bake for 25 minutes, until the rolls are a rich golden brown. Remove from the oven and let cool on the baking sheet for 5 minutes before buttering the tops. I like to just rub a slightly softened stick of butter on the warm rolls, or you can melt the butter and brush it on. ✳

### ❶ Holiday Sweet Potato Rolls
Add ½ teaspoon ground cinnamon and ⅛ teaspoon freshly grated nutmeg to the dough with the first 2 cups of flour.

### ❷ Roasted Garlic Potato Rolls
Use russet potatoes. Add 2 tablespoons roasted garlic to the dough mixture when you mix in the potatoes.

### ❸ Rainbow Rolls
If you're feeding a crowd, make one batch using each type of potato (russet, sweet, and purple). Then intermix the different types of dough balls on your baking sheets. The mixing of the flavors and colors is a mouth-dropping stunner.

❋

# Meatball Muffins

### (a juicy meatball in a muffin blanket)

yields 12 muffins

This is a dude's muffin—a hearty meatball, baked into a sauce-and-herb-spiced flaky muffin. A "meatball in a blanket," if you will . . . but cooler than that. A badass baller meal in a muffin.

### For the down and dirty meatballs:

1 pound lean ground beef

½ cup ricotta

¼ cup grated Parmesan cheese

½ teaspoon garlic salt

½ teaspoon onion salt

¼ teaspoon freshly ground black pepper

1 large egg

¼ cup plain breadcrumbs

2 tablespoons finely chopped fresh parsley

2 teaspoons finely chopped fresh oregano

2 teaspoons finely chopped fresh basil

### For the muffins:

⅔ cup prepared marinara sauce
(one with lots of garlic and herbs), plus more for dipping

2 large eggs

¼ cup vegetable oil

½ cup shredded mozzarella cheese

¾ cup grated Parmesan cheese

2 tablespoons chopped fresh herbs, such as parsley, basil, and oregano, or whatever you have handy

2 ½ cups all-purpose flour

1 ½ teaspoons baking powder

½ teaspoon salt

❶ **Make the down and dirty meatballs:** Preheat the oven to 350° F. Line a baking sheet with parchment paper or foil and set aside.

❷ In a large mixing bowl, mix all the ingredients well using your hands and form into 12 meatballs. Place on the prepared baking sheet and bake for 10 minutes. The meatballs will not be fully cooked. (They will bake again in the muffins.) Allow the meatballs to cool on the baking sheet while you prepare the muffin batter. Leave the oven on.

❸ **Make the muffin batter:** Spray a 12-cup muffin tin with nonstick cooking spray and set aside.

❹ In a medium mixing bowl, stir together the marinara sauce, eggs, oil, mozzarella, ¼ cup of the Parmesan, and the herbs. Set aside.

❺ In a large mixing bowl, whisk together the flour, baking powder, and salt. Stir the marinara mixture into the flour until completely combined. Fill each muffin tin cup about half full with batter, then place one cooled meatball into the center of the batter with the top of the meatball sticking up. Sprinkle the muffins with the remaining Parmesan and bake for 20 to 25 minutes, until golden brown. Serve warm with warm marinara sauce for dipping. ❋

*Wrap Meatball Muffins in plastic wrap or keep them in an airtight container in the refrigerator and they will last for up to 5 days. Bring the muffins to room temperature before eating. My husband and son like these better at room temperature than warm, whereas I like them warm. Sometimes I wonder if we really are related.*

✳

# Bob's Fried Firecracker

## (crunchy spicy saltines)

### yields 16 crackers

A strikingly handsome man of advanced age, Bob Patrick still has a fire in his eyes and a talent for colorful storytelling. Bob claims he grew up poor. He tells stories of having to catch fish so he and his two brothers would not go hungry; how, if it were a lucky day, one piece of fried bologna would feed four. My favorite stories involve what Bob calls "poor people food"— the most essential example of which is fried crackers. Bob says he could make a box of saltines and a stick of butter last through a week of after-school snacks for himself and his brothers—simply by frying them the right way.

And so begins the "Bob Patrick Cooking Show": "Not all crackers are the same." Bob insists on Nabisco Premium Saltines. "Salted butter only." I've seen Bob put salt on cantaloupe. "You can flip the cracker only once." Bob chases the crackers around the skillet with his index finger and thumb. "Timing is everything. You have to remove the crackers just when they begin to brown." Bob burns two. These days, whenever we share this snack, I can't help thinking that the man sitting next to me, wearing a suit worth more than my car, has come a long way from the memory of his youth. My favorite firecracker is Bob Patrick. Bob Patrick is my dad.

1 cup all-purpose flour, plus more for dusting

½ teaspoon salt, preferably a smoked salt

¼ teaspoon baking soda

5 tablespoons butter, melted

4 to 8 tablespoons cold water

1 ½ tablespoons hot chili sauce

½ teaspoon garlic salt

4 tablespoons vegetable oil

❶ In the bowl of a food processor, put the flour, salt, and baking soda. Pulse twice to combine. Add 1 tablespoon of the butter and pulse. Add 4 tablespoons cold water and pulse. Continue to add 1 tablespoon water at a time, pulsing after each addition, until the dough forms a slightly wet ball. Remove the blade from the food processor and let the dough rest in the bowl for 30 minutes.

❷ Preheat the oven to 375° F. Line a baking sheet with parchment paper and set aside.

❸ Turn the dough out onto a floured work surface and roll out to ¹⁄₁₆ inch thick—very thin. With a knife or fluted cutter, cut into 2-inch squares and place them on the baking sheet ⅛ inch apart (crackers won't spread). Re-roll the dough scraps as needed and cut more crackers. Prick the tops of the crackers with a skewer. (Bob insists on the traditional 3-2-3-2-3: Starting from the top, poke three holes across, then center two holes under the three, then three holes under the two and so on.) Bake for 8 to 10 minutes, until just barely browned on the edges. Allow to cool.

❹ In a medium mixing bowl, whisk together the remaining butter, hot chili sauce, and garlic salt. Add the crackers and toss gently to coat. Allow the crackers to remain in this spicy butter mixture for 15 minutes.

❺ Heat half the oil in a large sauté pan over medium heat. Working in two batches, fry the crackers for 5 minutes, until just brown on one side, then turn and fry for another 5 minutes, until the second side is just brown and remove to a serving plate. Use the remaining oil to fry the second batch. Serve warm or at room temperature. ✳

*How do you serve Bob's Fried Firecrackers? Float them on a bowl of soup, scoop them into a wide-mouth jar of pimento cheese, or top them with a piece of fried bologna—it's what Bob Patrick would do.*

show & tell

# Pull-Apart Boy Bread

## (1 dough, 5 recipe variations) yields 1 loaf

I'm an expert on boys. They are my thing. Most of my friends are boys. In the past I've dated boys from six continents (it would be seven, but no one dates anyone from Antarctica). I am married to a boy and my only child is a boy. In my life study of boys, I've found that most boys have the same basic make-up. It's when you pull apart the layers that their true personality shines. Much like this bread.

2 cups all-purpose flour, plus more for dusting

2 teaspoons baking powder

½ teaspoon baking soda

1 teaspoon salt

½ teaspoon freshly ground black pepper

½ cup (1 stick) butter, cubed, plus 2 tablespoons melted butter

1 cup buttermilk

1 recipe Boy Filling (choices follow on page 96)

Preheat the oven to 425° F. Spray a 9-by-5-inch loaf pan with nonstick cooking spray and set aside.

In the bowl of a food processor, pulse the flour with the baking powder, baking soda, salt, and pepper. Add the cubed butter and pulse until the flour mixture forms pea-size pieces. Add the buttermilk and pulse just until a soft dough forms. Turn the dough out onto a well-floured work surface and knead it gently three times.

## How To Assemble Pull-Apart Boy Bread

1 Roll the dough out into a long thin rectangle (about 8 by 24 inches).

2 Brush the top of the dough with 1 tablespoon of the melted butter.

3 Spread with your choice of toppings and press the toppings into the dough slightly.

4 Using a sharp knife, cut the dough in half lengthwise.

*continued on page 96*

show & tell

## Pull-Apart Boy Bread, continued

# Boy Filling Options

### Stinky Italian Boy

Cook 12 garlic cloves over medium-low heat in ¼ cup olive oil for about 30 minutes, until golden brown, then let cool and mash the garlic. Combine with 2 tablespoons chopped fresh Italian herbs (your choice) and 1 cup grated Parmesan cheese.

### Bourgeois Boy

Cut 1 Vidalia or other sweet yellow onion into thin strips and cook with 2 tablespoons butter and ¼ teaspoon beef base in a medium skillet over low heat for 15 minutes, or until the onion is soft and caramel-colored. Let cool. Stir together the caramelized onion and 1 cup shredded Gruyère cheese.

### Cute Greek Boy

Stir together 1 cup chopped Kalamata olives, 1 tablespoon chopped fresh dill, and 1 cup crumbled feta cheese.

### Pretty Boy

Stir together 2 tablespoons honey, ½ cup chopped toasted walnuts, ¼ cup chopped dried pears, and 3 ounces blue cheese.

### Eagle Scout Boy

Stir together 1 tablespoon poppy seeds, 1 tablespoon toasted sesame seeds, ⅓ cup sunflower seeds, and ⅓ cup pepitas (hulled pumpkin seeds).

**5** Cut the dough widthwise into nine equal-size strips. You will have eighteen equal pieces of dough.

**6** Stack all but one piece of the dough on top of each other with the toppings facing up. Place the final piece on the top with the toppings facing down. The dough is sticky enough that the stack will hold together when pressed a little. Don't worry: This is going to get messy and that's okay.

**7** Carefully lay the stack on its side in the prepared loaf pan (the filling of the two ends will not touch the pan). Sprinkle any of the contents that may have fallen out onto the top of the dough once it's in the pan. Separate the slices a little with your fingertips once they are in the pan and brush the top with the remaining 1 tablespoon butter.

**8** Bake the loaf for 30 minutes, until it has risen and is golden brown. Let the bread cool slightly before removing from the pan and serving.

# Border Guard Sausage Biscuits

### (gigantic hot pepper sausage, two cheese biscuits)

#### yields 6

Cheesy gigantic biscuits wrapped around a spicy pork sausage that could easily feed two, these biscuits are the perfect head-turning temptation. I have imagined that, when and if I ever have to escape this country, these sausage biscuits may persuade a hungry border guard to look the other way . . . at least in Canada.

This is a perfect make-ahead recipe. Both the biscuits and the sausage patties can be made a day in advance and put together whenever you need them. Just refrigerate the cooked patties, then bring to room temperature when you're ready to serve. Put a little vegetable oil in a skillet over medium-low heat and cook the patties for about 5 minutes, or until they're heated through. Keep the biscuits in a zip-top bag overnight at room temperature. There's no need to heat them again. The heat from the sausage will warm them right up.

**For the biscuits:**

4 cups all-purpose flour, plus more for dusting

4 teaspoons baking powder

1 teaspoon baking soda

1 teaspoon salt

1 teaspoon sugar

¼ cup (½ stick) cold butter, cubed, plus 3 tablespoons melted butter

¾ cup cold leaf lard (see Note; you may substitute vegetable shortening, but I won't be happy about it)

1 cup shredded cheddar cheese

2 cups shredded pepper Jack cheese

2 cups cold buttermilk

**For the sausage patties:**

2 tablespoons vegetable oil

½ large sweet onion, finely diced

2 garlic cloves, minced

2 (4-ounce) cans chopped green chiles

1 teaspoon freshly ground black pepper

1 ½ pounds ground pork breakfast sausage, casings removed

**To serve:**

3 tablespoons mustard

6 fried eggs (optional)

*Leaf lard is the lard rendered from the fat that deposits around a pig's kidney and inside the loin. It's perfect for use in baking as it has little or no pork flavor. Leaf lard has been my fat of choice ever since I learned to render it when I was a little girl on my grandparents' Missouri hog farm.*

**❶ Make the biscuits:** Preheat the oven to 375° F. Line a baking sheet with parchment paper and set aside.

**❷** In a large mixing bowl, whisk together the flour, baking powder, baking soda, salt, and sugar. Using two forks, a pastry blender, or your cold hands (run them under cold water), cut in the cubed butter and the lard until the mixture resembles large breadcrumbs. You should still see chunks of butter in the dough. Stir in both cheeses. Add the buttermilk and stir just until the mixture comes together (it will still be pretty wet). Lightly flour your hands and a work surface and turn the dough out onto the surface. Pat the dough out to 1 inch thick. Using a 5-inch round cutter dipped in flour, cut out six biscuits. Place the biscuits on the prepared baking sheet and brush the tops with the melted butter. Bake for 20 to 24 minutes, until lightly browned. Let the biscuits cool slightly before splitting.

**❸ While the biscuits are baking, make the sausage patties:** In a medium sauté pan over medium-low heat, heat 1 tablespoon of the oil and sauté the onion for 4 minutes. Stir in the garlic and cook for 1 minute. Stir in the chiles and black pepper and cook for 1 minute. Set the mixture aside until it is cool enough to handle.

**❹** Put the pork sausage in a medium mixing bowl and use your hands to mix in the chile mixture. Divide the sausage into six equal portions and shape each into a 5-inch disc.

**❺** Heat the remaining 1 tablespoon oil in a large sauté pan. Working in two batches, cook the sausage patties for 5 to 8 minutes per side, turning once, until they are browned and cooked through. Transfer to a plate and cover with foil to keep warm while cooking the remaining patties (you shouldn't need any fresh oil for the pan).

**❻** Spread mustard on the bottom halves of the biscuits and top each with a warm sausage patty. If you like, you can also add a fried or scrambled egg on top of the sausage patty. Serve warm. *

*Savory Breads*

✳

# Campfire Bread

### (rosemary, black olives, + glowing embers)

yields 2 loaves

A chic campfire bread.

Mix the dough at your campsite or feel free to mix it before you leave your house and bake it after you pitch your tent.

5 cups bread flour, plus more for dusting

1 ½ teaspoons smoked salt

1 ½ teaspoons active dry yeast

1 tablespoon chopped fresh rosemary

⅔ cup black olives, roughly chopped (large chunks)

❶ **Campfire-cooking method:** In a large mixing bowl using a dough whisk, whisk together the flour, smoked salt, and yeast. Add 1¾ cups water and mix until the dough is a messy, ugly ball. Exchange the dough whisk for your hands and start kneading in the bowl. Once the dough begins to get firm, add the rosemary and olives and work them into the dough. Cover the bowl with plastic wrap and let the dough rest for 1 hour.

❷ Remove the dough from the bowl, cut it into two equal parts, and shape each part into a round. Place one dough round in a lidded cast-iron Dutch oven. (Don't be tempted to use your favorite Le Creuset here . . . it will never be the same. Especially when the handle melts from the hot coals. Always use a good old black cast-iron pot and lid. Always.) Wrap the other in a plastic bag and reserve in a cooler until the next day (just punch it down and shape it into a round when you are ready to bake). Cover the Dutch oven and let the dough rest for 1 to 1½ hours, until it has doubled in size.

❸ While your dough is rising, build a medium-size fire with coal or wood and burn until it is very hot (no flames and the coals are glowing). Spread the coals out to form a circle a little larger than the circumference of the Dutch oven.

❹ Using a sharp paring knife, score the top of the dough by cutting an X into the top and cover with a lid.

❺ Place three rocks in the coals for the Dutch oven to sit on and transfer the Dutch oven to the fire. Carefully scoop up 10 to 12 hot coals and place them on the lid of the oven (this will help bake the bread evenly, top and bottom). Bake for 40 minutes, until the dough is golden brown and crisp and sounds hollow when you knock on it. When removing the lid to check on doneness, be careful you don't get ash on your bread.

*continued on page 102*

*continued on page 102*

❶ **Home-cooking method:** In the bowl of a standing mixer fitted with the whisk attachment, combine the flour, smoked salt, and yeast and stir to combine. Add 1¾ cups water and mix until the dough is a messy, ugly ball.

❷ Replace the whisk attachment with a dough hook and mix the dough for 4 minutes, or until it's firm and smooth. Add the rosemary and olives and mix until they are distributed evenly throughout the dough. Cover the dough and let rest for 1 hour.

❸ Turn the dough out onto a lightly floured surface. Cut it into two equal parts and shape them into rounds. Cover and let the dough rest for 1 to 1½ hours, until it has doubled in size. (I like to use proofing baskets for this stage; if you don't have one, no worries, just place on a parchment-lined baking sheet. If you do, dust two baskets with flour and shake out any excess. Place one round of dough, top side down, in each basket and allow them to rise until they have doubled in size.)

❹ Preheat the oven to 450° F. Place a cast-iron skillet or steam pan in the bottom of the oven, and a baking stone or baking sheet in the middle of the oven to preheat.

❺ Score the tops of the loaves and place them on the baking stone or baking sheet. (If using a proofing basket, turn the basket over and gently remove the loaves from the basket before scoring the top.) Add 1 cup of ice cubes to the cast-iron skillet and close the oven door. Bake for 20 minutes, then lower the oven temperature to 425° F and continue to bake for 20 minutes, or until the bread is a rich brown color. Let cool completely before slicing or tearing. ❋

Things that should come out of a box: crayons, matches, cheap wine, and pills.

Things that should never come out of a box: cake and cornbread.

✳

# Kickin' Cornbread

### (skillet-baked + drenched in spicy bacon butter)

serves 8

2 thick slices bacon

6 tablespoons butter

1 large jalapeño chile, minced (remove the seeds and membranes if you can't stand the heat)

2 garlic cloves, minced

1 ½ cups stone-ground yellow cornmeal

1 teaspoon baking soda

1 teaspoon sugar

½ teaspoon salt

½ teaspoon ground cayenne

2 large eggs, at room temperature

1 ¾ cups buttermilk, at room temperature

Juice of ½ lemon

1 scallion (green and white parts), chopped

❶ Preheat the oven to 425° F.

❷ In a 10-inch cast-iron skillet over medium heat, fry the bacon until crisp and drain on a paper towel–lined plate. Finely chop the bacon and set it aside. Reduce the heat under the skillet to low and add 3 tablespoons of the butter to the rendered bacon fat. Stir in the chile and garlic and cook, stirring, for 1 minute. Using a slotted spoon, transfer the jalapeño and garlic to a small saucepan. Turn off the heat and swirl the butter and rendered bacon fat around the skillet and up the sides to coat.

❸ In a large mixing bowl, whisk together the cornmeal, baking soda, sugar, salt, and cayenne.

❹ In a separate mixing bowl, whisk the eggs and buttermilk until blended.

❺ Pour the warm butter and rendered bacon fat mixture from the skillet into the cornmeal mixture (leaving a little in the pan) and put the empty skillet into the oven to heat while you mix the rest of the batter. Add the buttermilk mixture to the cornmeal mixture. Working quickly, stir the batter just until it's moistened. Remove the hot skillet from the oven and scrape the batter into it. Bake for 10 minutes, or until the cornbread is golden brown around the edges.

❻ While the cornbread is baking, add the remaining 3 tablespoons butter and the lemon juice to the small saucepan with the jalapeño and garlic. Melt the butter over low heat, remove from the heat, and stir in the scallion and bacon. Spoon the mixture over the hot baked cornbread and allow it to soak in for a couple of minutes before eating. Slice and serve straight from the skillet. ✳

✳

# Flat-Chested Flat Bread

### (grilled, sweet, spicy, + cheesy)

#### yields 8

A training bread, if you will. A soft, chewy, simple bread grilled and brought alive with the sweet heat of brown sugar and chile oil. A bread to honor flat-chested girls everywhere. I was once one of you . . . spicy, sweet, and just waiting to rise.

1 tablespoon vegetable oil, plus more for the grill

3 cups warm water

2 ½ teaspoons active dry yeast

5 cups all-purpose flour

2 cups whole wheat flour

2 tablespoons salt

½ cup plain Greek yogurt

4 teaspoons chile oil (available in the international section of your grocery store)

4 teaspoons brown sugar

¼ cup grated Parmesan cheese

❶ In the bowl of a standing mixer fitted with the dough hook, combine the 1 tablespoon vegetable oil with the water. Add the yeast and stir to dissolve. Cover and let rest for 30 minutes.

❷ Add the all-purpose and whole wheat flours to the yeast mixture and mix on low speed just until a loose, raggedy dough forms. Cover the bowl of the mixer and let the dough rest for 20 minutes.

❸ Add the salt and yogurt to the dough and mix for 5 minutes, until the ingredients are fully incorporated and the dough pulls away from the sides of the bowl to form a loose ball. Remove the dough hook, cover the bowl with plastic wrap, and let rise at room temperature for 3 to 4 hours, until the dough has doubled in size.

❹ Preheat an outdoor gas or charcoal grill to high.

❺ Turn the dough out onto a generously floured work surface. Divide the dough into eight equal portions and roll out each portion to ¼ inch thick (or press with your hands). Don't worry about uniformity: the less perfect, the better. Stack the dough rounds on the bottom of an overturned baking sheet, placing a sheet of oiled plastic wrap between them so they won't stick together.

❻ Brush the grill liberally with oil and, working two at a time, grill the flatbreads for 2 to 3 minutes per side, until there is a nice black/brown char on the grill side and the top is puffing up. If the dough sticks to the grill when you try to turn it, the flatbread has not cooked long enough.

❼ When the flatbreads are hot off the grill, drizzle them lightly with chile oil (a little goes a long way) and sprinkle with a little brown sugar and cheese. Serve warm. ✳

*I like to top my flatbreads with just about anything I have in the refrigerator—from olives and radishes to bacon. The only constant when it comes to toppings I like is the Parmesan cheese. I always make it cheesy.*

show & tell

# Pretzel Bread

**(a sliceable hot pretzel)** yields 2 loaves, or twelve 4-inch rolls

½ cup plus 2 tablespoons warm water (115° F)

½ cup warm milk

3 tablespoons butter, melted

2 ½ teaspoons active dry yeast

3 tablespoons packed dark brown sugar

1 teaspoon salt, plus more for sprinkling

3 cups bread flour, plus more for dusting

¼ teaspoon vegetable oil

½ cup baking soda

I think it was in fifth grade that I studied states and capitals. Each student's final grade depended on an oral presentation about an "adopted" state. Our teacher wrote all the states on colorful pieces of paper and placed them in a goldfish bowl for us to choose. I picked Montana. It could have been worse; my friend Randy picked Idaho. I don't remember much about the presentations aside from the Missouri one given by my classmate Paul, who had a talent for the theatrical. Paul donned a coonskin cap as he talked about Daniel Boone, then deftly removed the cap and taped on a white felt mustache as he read a poem by Mark Twain. The best part of Paul's state performance was the German pretzel bread he passed around as he talked about Germans immigrating to St. Louis in the mid-1800s. The bread was the best thing I had ever eaten inside the walls of our school. Still warm from Paul's book bag, it tasted like a thick slice of pretzel. I've been obsessed with it—and Paul—ever since. I hope Paul earned an A on his presentation. He deserved it for the bread alone. I'll ask him the next time we talk. All these years later, Paul and I are still the best of friends.

**1** In the bowl of a standing mixer fitted with the dough hook, put the water, milk, butter, yeast, and brown sugar. Mix until combined, then let the mixture rest for 10 minutes, or until it begins to foam. Mix in the salt.

**2** With the mixer on low speed, add 2 cups of the flour and mix for 1 minute. Continue to add the remaining flour as needed until the dough forms a firm ball that is tacky, not sticky (think about a Post-it note—it's tacky, not sticky to the touch). Transfer the dough to a mixing bowl. Drizzle the dough ball with the oil and turn it over in the bowl to coat. Cover with plastic wrap and let the dough rise at room temperature for 30 minutes.

**3** Knead the dough at medium-low speed for 10 minutes, until the dough has a satiny shine and is elastic. Cover the dough and let rise for 1 hour, or until it doubles in size. At this point, if you would like to make Pretzel Brats see the variation on page 110.

**4** Turn the dough out onto a lightly floured work surface and divide into two equal pieces. Roll each piece between the palms of your hand in a circular motion to form two smooth balls. (If making rolls, divide the dough into twelve equal pieces and form into balls, then continue with the following steps.)

*continued on page 108*

## Pretzel Bread, continued

**5** Preheat the oven to 400° F. Line a baking sheet with parchment paper and set aside. In a stockpot, bring 4 quarts water to a boil. Slowly add the baking soda without stirring.

**6** Working with one dough ball at a time, use a large spider or slotted spoon to slowly lower the dough ball into the boiling water. Boil for 30 seconds, turning once to make sure the complete surface of the dough has been covered with water. Remove with the slotted spoon to drain and transfer to the prepared baking sheet. Repeat with the second ball of dough.

**7** Make a cross in the top of each loaf using a sharp knife or razor. Don't worry if the dough looks rather ugly at this point; it will pop up and become beautiful during baking.

**8** Sprinkle the loaves with salt (kosher, pretzel, or Maldon salt). I like a salty pretzel bread and salt-free pretzel rolls.

**9** Bake for 25 minutes (15 minutes for rolls), until the loaves are a dark golden brown, turning the baking sheet around once in the middle of the bake time. Let the loaves cool slightly before serving.

*Things I love about Germans: 1,000 different kinds of sausages, Ludwig Mies van der Rohe, gooey butter cake, Katarina Witt, Gummi Bears, Karl Lagerfeld, Mozart, a 1987 325ic BMW Convertible (bronzette gold, named Evelyn), and Pretzel Bread.*

\*

# Pretzel Brats

## (a beer-bathed brat wrapped in a pretzel)

yields 6

6 bratwurst

12 ounces pale ale

¼ cup (½ stick) butter

1 onion, sliced

1 teaspoon freshly ground black pepper

1 recipe Pretzel Bread dough (prepared through step 3)

½ cup baking soda

Kosher or sea salt

6 tablespoons spicy mustard

❶ Bring 4 cups water to a simmer in a medium saucepan over medium heat and add the bratwurst, ale, butter, onion, and pepper. Cook for 25 minutes, then drain the bratwurst.

❷ Prepare a gas or charcoal grill for cooking over direct heat, or preheat a grill pan over medium-high heat. Sear the brats, turning, for 2 to 3 minutes. Let cool completely. (If you're in a hurry, don't bother to grill the brats. They are already cooked; the grilling just adds another layer of flavor and crunch.)

❸ Preheat the oven to 400° F. Line a baking sheet with parchment paper and set aside.

❹ In a large saucepan, bring 4 quarts water to a boil over high heat and slowly add the baking soda.

❺ On a lightly floured work surface, turn out the dough and lightly pat it out to a flat disc. Divide the dough into 6 equal portions and roll each portion into a flat rope about 12 inches long by 1 inch wide. Wrap one rope around each bratwurst, leaving both ends of the sausage exposed.

❻ Working with one brat at a time, use a large spider or slotted spoon to slowly lower the brat into the boiling water and boil for 30 seconds, turning once to make sure the complete surface of the dough has been covered with water. Remove and allow the excess water to drain before placing the brat on the baking sheet. Repeat with the remaining brats. Sprinkle the brats with salt and bake for 20 to 25 minutes, until dark brown. Serve with mustard. \*

✳

# Forgiveness Naan

### (pillowy garlic butter flatbread)

#### yields 10

Naan is my yeast-based guilty pleasure. Wherever I may be traveling in the world, I'm searching for this pillowy flatbread with the crisp bottom. If there is a restaurant with naan on the menu, mark my words, I will find it.

Although I have yet to taste dreamy Chef Suvir Saran's naan (he promises to make me some one day), my favorite naan is made at a seedy back-alley restaurant in the West Indies by a guy named Sanjay (come to think of it, most of the naan bakers I've met are named Sanjay). I've been lucky enough to land on Sanjay's island many times over the years while cooking on boats. Even luckier, he has always been around, is always wearing too much cologne, and is always willing to bake me a fresh basketful of naan—no matter what time of day. Each piece of Sanjay's naan is the size of a roadmap, spilling over the sides of the basket of bread he brings to the table. It has the perfect charred bottom and buttery flavor . . . with just a hint of Old Spice.

Once you start baking your own naan, you'll quickly discover what all Sanjay naan bakers already know: Naan gets better every time you make it. Like an elastic waistband, the dough is very forgiving.

6 tablespoons clarified butter (page 209), melted

1 teaspoon active dry yeast

1 teaspoon brown sugar

1 ¼ cups warm milk (110° F)

3 tablespoons plain whole-milk yogurt

1 teaspoon salt

3 to 4 cups all-purpose flour, sifted, plus more for dusting

2 tablespoons minced garlic

❶ Use a small bit of the clarified butter to lightly grease a large mixing bowl. Set aside.

❷ In the bowl of a standing mixer fitted with the paddle attachment, combine the yeast, brown sugar, and milk. Briefly stir with a spoon. Let the mixture rest for 5 minutes, or until it begins to foam. With the mixer on low speed, add the yogurt, 2 tablespoons of the clarified butter, and the salt. Add the flour, starting with 2 cups and mixing well to combine. Gradually add enough flour until the dough forms and cleanly pull away from the sides of the mixing bowl. Mix for 5 minutes, or until the dough is smooth and elastic.

❸ Put the dough in the greased mixing bowl, cover, and let it rest at room temperature for 1½ to 2 hours, until it has doubled in size.

❹ Turn the dough out onto a lightly floured surface and divide it into ten equal portions. Use your palms to form each into a ball. Cover the dough balls with a towel and let rest for 30 minutes.

❺ Preheat the oven to 500° F. Position one oven rack on the lowest level of the oven and remove or place the other rack high enough in the oven to stay out of your way. Place a baking stone (or pizza stone) on the lowest rack. Have a spray bottle of water and a cooling rack ready.

❻ Stir the garlic into the remaining butter.

❼ Roll each piece of dough out (or pat the dough out with your hands and fingertips) to an 8- to 10-inch circle. Pull one end of the dough to form a teardrop shape. Brush the dough lightly with the garlic butter. Working with one shaped piece of dough at a time, carefully place it on the hot baking stone and spritz the dough with water. Bake for about 4 minutes, until brown spots start to form on top and the dough begins to puff up. Remove the naan from the oven and brush again lightly with the garlic butter. Repeat the process with the remaining pieces of dough, keeping the cooked naan covered and warm until ready to serve. At my house, the naan doesn't stand a chance of getting cold. Every piece seems to disappear as soon as it comes out of the oven. ✳

\*

# Napoleon Bread

## (a shorter baguette)

### yields 4 loaves

I put my baguettes in the refrigerator overnight to do a cold fermentation. It's less messy and I think the dough holds its shape better . . . and those are the only reasons why. The taste is the same. The only thing to be cautious about is not to use too much pressure when you do the final shaping of the refrigerated dough—like a short Frenchman, you don't want to squeeze out all the hot air/gas.

2 cups warm water (about 95° F)

2 ½ teaspoons active dry yeast

1 tablespoon salt

5 ½ cups bread flour, plus more for dusting

Vegetable oil, for the bowl

❶ In the bowl of a standing mixer fitted with the paddle attachment, put the water and yeast and stir until just combined. Add the salt and flour and mix on low speed just until the dough forms an ugly ball. Switch to the dough hook and mix on medium speed for 2 minutes, until the dough is smooth and tacky, but not too sticky (see Note). You can adjust the flour or water here as needed. (If the dough is too dry, add water, 1 tablespoon at a time. If the dough is too wet, add more bread flour, 1 tablespoon at a time.) Let the dough rest in the bowl for 5 minutes.

❷ Oil the inside of a large mixing bowl with the oil and set aside.

❸ Turn the dough out onto a lightly floured work surface and knead by hand for 1 minute. Transfer the dough to the oiled mixing bowl, cover the bowl with plastic wrap, and refrigerate overnight. Punch the dough down with your fist if it starts creeping over the top of the bowl.

❹ Remove the dough from the refrigerator about 2 hours before you want to bake the loaves. Being careful not to deflate the dough too much, transfer it to a lightly floured surface and divide into four equal portions.

❺ Line a baking sheet with a large kitchen towel that has been lightly dusted with flour. Set aside.

❻ Form the four dough portions into baguettes by first shaping the dough into a thick rectangle about 14 by 6 inches. Fold the bottom half of the longer side of the rectangle to the center of the dough and press with your fingers to hold it in place. Next fold the top half to the center and press it with your fingertips to seal the seam you have created. Roll the bottom of the dough over the top, creating a new seam on the underside. Gently rock the dough back and forth while moving your hands out toward both ends. This lengthens the baguette. Apply a little more pressure at the ends to taper the dough slightly. Repeat the rocking motion as many times as necessary until the baguette is about 16 inches long by 2½ inches wide.

**7** Transfer the baguette to the floured cloth and repeat the shaping process with the remaining pieces of dough. Tuck folds of the floured cloth around the sides of the loaves to help support the dough as it rises and to help separate the baguettes. Oil the underside of a piece of plastic wrap and loosely cover the loaves with it. Let sit at room temperature for 90 minutes, until the loaves have not quite doubled in size. The dough will increase 1½ to 1¾ times in size. (As with many things in life, here size does matter.)

**8** About 45 minutes before baking, preheat your oven as high as it will go. Place a baking stone or an overturned heavy-duty baking sheet on the middle rack of the oven and place a cast-iron skillet on the lowest shelf or on the floor of the oven.

**9** Remove the plastic wrap from the dough. Using a sharp razor or serrated knife at a 30-degree angle to the loaf, make 4 or 5 equidistant slashes, 4 inches long and ½ inch deep, in the top of each baguette. Transfer each baguette to the hot baking stone or baking sheet (don't worry if they collapse a bit, they will spring back while baking). Spritz the baguettes lightly with water and place 1 cup ice cubes in the cast-iron skillet.

**10** Lower the oven temperature to 450° F. Bake the baguettes for 30 minutes, or until the crust is a dark golden brown and the loaves sound hollow if you give them a thump. Let cool for at least 30 minutes before serving. ✳

*Don't try to double this recipe using a regular standing mixer. This is the maximum amount of dough my home mixer can handle.*

*When I use the term tacky in a recipe, think about a Post-it note, how it feels when you put your finger on it. It's tacky not sticky.*

✳

# Monet's Favorite Sandwich

### (warm roasted chicken, brie, + raspberry jam on baguette)

serves 4

My obsession with the dining habits of Claude Monet began in college. I feasted again and again on the few English translations available of the notebooks he kept from his home in Giverny. At a time when my cooking skills were constrained by the size of my dorm room hotplate and my wallet, I would dream about the elaborate lunches Monet held promptly at 11:30 each day for guests like Renoir, Cézanne, and Degas. Some of the local ingredients that were mentioned in the notebooks included capons, chickens, berries, cheeses, and wonderful breads.

It wasn't long after that I started making what I call Monet's Favorite Sandwich. I thought: What if he was a sandwich eater and he put some of his favorite ingredients together between sliced bread? Wouldn't it make the best sandwich in the world?

And it did.

I've yet to meet anyone who doesn't love this sandwich. It has everything. Savory chicken, sweet raspberry preserves, creamy/salty brie, and the yeasty crunch of a baguette. Like Monet himself, this sandwich is kind of sweet and vicious. In the past, when someone asked me for the recipe, I told them to read Monet's notebooks from Giverny. Now I'm a little sad thinking they may not have done so.

1 loaf Napoleon Bread (page 116),
or your favorite baguette, split in half lengthwise

¼ cup raspberry preserves

½ small roasted chicken, bones removed
and meat sliced or torn into large pieces

4 ounces brie

Fresh parsley leaves (optional)

❶ Preheat the broiler.

❷ Line a baking sheet with parchment paper and place the bottom half of the bread on it. Spread the raspberry preserves over the bread. Top the preserves with the chicken. Cut the brie into chunks or slices and spread across the top of the chicken. Broil for 3 to 5 minutes, until the cheese is just melted. Top with parsley if you like. Place the top half of the bread on the sandwich and cut into four equal pieces. Serve warm. ✳

\*

# Open Face Radish & Olive Butter Sandwich
## (crisp baguette topped with salty butter + spicy radishes)
### serves 4

The students of St. John's College in Annapolis, Maryland, study the works of great thinkers such as Homer, Du Bois, and Woolf. A little less than fifty feet to the north, the uniformed midshipmen of the United States Naval Academy have a curriculum that includes the study of applied sciences and those courses required to become an officer of the U.S. Navy. Though such a short distance from each other, the two schools and their student bodies are worlds apart. Each year, on a Saturday in late April, the playing field is leveled when the two schools compete in one gentlemen's sport—croquet.

The first time I tasted a sandwich of radish and butter was not in the French countryside, it was on the manicured grounds of St. John's College, the day of the annual croquet match with Navy. I was sitting on a steamer chair and wearing an antique white dress and voile hat, with my equally costumed mother-in-law, Peggy (an Annapolitan who still dreams of being a Parisian), seated next to me. The picnic basket Peggy prepared for our lunch consisted of two radish and butter sandwiches and one bottle of rosé. Peggy and I were two of a crowd of hundreds who all looked like we'd stepped out of a Seurat painting while listening to a four-piece band and enjoying a celebratory truce.

It was the one day out of the year where two very different schools put down their books and swords and raised a striped croquet mallet in unity.

½ cup (1 stick) butter, at room temperature

¼ cup chopped Kalamata olives

1 loaf Napoleon Bread (page 116),
or your favorite baguette, split in half lengthwise

4 large radishes with tops, greens cleaned and dried

Maldon or kosher salt

❶ In a small bowl, stir together the butter and olives. Spread the mixture over both cut sides of the bread.

❷ Remove the leaves from the radishes and discard the stems. Very thinly slice the radishes and spread them over the olive butter on both sides of the bread. Top with the radish leaves and sprinkle with salt. Cut each half of bread into two pieces. \*

*This is a perfect picnic sandwich. Pack all the ingredients separately and assemble when you get to your destination. Don't forget to pack a bread knife.*

# Boat Bagels

### (perfect chewy dough, garlic bacon topping)

#### yields 12 bagels

Keith was a modern-day pirate. An elusive yacht captain with a big ego and the background to back it up. In his prime, Keith ran sailing yachts for the rich and famous. When he is rum-fueled, he can fill weeks with stories of partying with royals, drug runs from South America, fishing with presidents and dictators, and the twelve days he spent on a life raft.

When I first met Keith, he was near the end of his sailing career, content to be running and living aboard a private midsized sailboat. For a period of three months, my husband and ten-year-old son and I cruised on our modest forty-foot sailboat in the same area of the Lesser Antilles as Keith—but we were worlds apart. Keith's boat had refrigeration, an endless supply of hot water, satellite television, and a pair of night vision goggles. Ours had none of those things. Time and again, we would anchor in a harbor near Keith's impeccably cared-for boat, but we rarely saw him.

Occasionally we would see Keith on deck—a handsome man in his fifties, with long graying hair that shone against his sun-darkened skin. He stood over six feet tall and weighed barely ten stones. Sick of each other in the small confines of our sailboat and hoping to have someone new to talk to, we would wave and say hello. Keith would nod back, but never wave or speak. Couldn't figure it out. Did he just think he was better than we were?

On a certain Sunday morning, anchored in Admiralty Bay off the island of Bequia, Keith's boat was just off our stern. I was determined to win this guy over and I decided to do it the only way I knew how—through his stomach. I got up early and made bagel dough. (Lucky for me, on a hot boat in the Caribbean, dough proofs quickly.) Before I started the boil and bake, the boys went over to see if Keith might want to join us for fresh bagels (thinking that no one on boat or land would ever turn down an invitation to eat). And I was right. I made a dozen bagels that morning, and the four of us ate ten. Three hours later Keith returned to his boat with the last two bagels, which I had wrapped up for him. Three hours and ten minutes later, he radioed over to see if we wanted to come take a hot shower and watch a movie.

Over the next two months, Keith would stop by our boat often for drinks, dinner, and story hour. He became a generous friend and even let our son play with his night vision goggles. We all laughed about his aloofness in the beginning and the power of a bagel. Keith was a good man.

I never saw Keith after that time in the Caribbean. I heard he left this life a few years later after living it to the fullest. I've probably made bagels a hundred times since making them for Keith off the coast of Bequia, and each time I think of him, how kind he was to my family . . . and the healing power of a bagel.

## Boat Bagels, continued

### For the dough:

2 tablespoons vegetable oil, for brushing

2 ¼ cups lukewarm water

2 teaspoons active dry yeast

2 tablespoons honey

1 tablespoon salt

7 cups bread flour, plus more for dusting

### For the garlic bacon topping:

6 garlic cloves

1 tablespoon olive oil

6 slices bacon, cooked until crisp, finely chopped

2 tablespoons toasted sesame seeds

1 tablespoon salt

### For the poaching liquid:

5 tablespoons honey

¼ cup baking soda

1 tablespoon plus 1 teaspoon salt

*You could skip the topping and make them plain, but I would prefer you didn't.*

**❶ Make the dough:** Brush the inside of an extra-large mixing bowl with the vegetable oil and set aside.

**❷** Pour the water into the bowl of a standing mixer fitted with the dough hook and add the yeast, honey, and salt. Let stand for 5 minutes, then stir to mix. Add the flour and mix on the lowest speed for 3 minutes, until well blended. The dough will be a stiff ball. Let the dough rest in the bowl for 5 minutes, then mix again on low speed for another 3 minutes.

**❸** Turn the dough out onto a lightly floured surface and knead by hand for 5 to 10 minutes, until the dough is barely tacky, has a satiny sheen, and is firm. If the dough is a little too wet at this point, knead in a bit more flour to get to make it firm.

**❹** Put the dough in the prepared mixing bowl and turn to coat it with the oil. Cover the bowl with plastic wrap and let the dough rise in a warm place for 1 hour, or until it has doubled in size. Punch the dough down and let it rest for another 10 minutes.

**❺** Line two baking sheets with parchment paper and set aside. Have a small bowl of water ready.

**❻** Divide the dough into twelve equal portions. Working with one piece of dough at a time, shape the dough into a loose ball by cupping it in your hand and rolling the dough on a clean, dry work surface in a circular motion just until a perfect ball forms. Using your finger, poke a hole through the center of the ball to create a donut shape.

**❼** Next, holding the dough with both thumbs in the hole (like learning to drive a car with your hands at the ten and two o'clock positions), rotate the dough with your hands, gradually stretching it to create a 2-inch-diameter hole in the center. Place the shaped bagel on a prepared baking sheet and repeat the process with the remaining pieces of dough, dividing them between the two baking sheets. Cover the bagels with plastic wrap that has been brushed with oil and refrigerate them overnight. Bagels can be made to this point and kept, covered with plastic wrap, for up to 2 days in the refrigerator.

**❽** Remove the bagels from the refrigerator and let them come to room temperature.

**❾** Preheat the oven to 500° F.

**❿ Make the garlic bacon topping:** Sauté the whole garlic cloves in the oil in a small skillet over medium heat for 3 to 4 minutes, until yellow gold, then drain on paper towels and chop finely. Put the garlic in a wide shallow baking dish, add the remaining ingredients, and toss together. Set aside.

**⓫ Make the poaching liquid:** In a large saucepan, bring 8 quarts water to a boil. Reduce the heat to maintain a simmer and stir in the honey, baking soda, and salt. Using a spider or slotted spoon, gently lower each bagel into the simmering liquid (you can poach 3 or 4 at a time). Poach the bagels for 1 minute, turn them over, and continue to poach for an additional 2 minutes. Remove the bagels from the water, allowing any excess water to drain off, and place them dome side up on the same parchment-lined baking sheet. Sprinkle with a generous amount of topping. Repeat with the remaining bagels.

**⓬** Transfer the baking sheets to the oven and lower the oven temperature to 475° F. Bake for 10 minutes, then rotate the pans and bake for another 5 minutes, or until a rich golden brown. Remove the bagels to a wire rack to cool for at least 30 minutes before serving. ✳

A pie
you crave.

# pies

*I'm a "don't refrigerate unless necessary" pie storage person. I lightly cover my fruit pies with plastic wrap and keep them at room temperature for up to two days. Savory pies I wrap tightly with plastic wrap and refrigerate for up to three days, allowing them to come to room temperature before serving.*

Opposite: Preggers Pink Pickle Pie, page 144

show & tell

# The Cold Truth Pie Dough

**(flaky with a little kick of sweet heat)** yields 1 double-crust pie

2 ½ cups all-purpose flour

1 tablespoon vanilla sugar (page 202)

½ teaspoon salt

¼ teaspoon ground cayenne

12 tablespoons cold unsalted butter, cubed

¼ cup cold lard (I prefer leaf lard) or vegetable shortening

4 to 8 tablespoons ice water

Cold is the key to the success of my award-winning pie dough. Cold bowl, cold hands, cold fat—and the cold truth. That pinch of heat and sweet? That's for the cold at heart.

(It's the magic of the butter and lard—the fat—that makes the flakiest crust. When the dough is heated, the fat melts and creates little pockets in the flour. The water content of the fat becomes steam that escapes and makes the little pockets puff up. The puffs are what make a dough flaky. No puff = no flake.)

*Leaf lard is the lard rendered from the fat that deposits around a pig's kidney and inside the loin. It's perfect for use in baking as it has little or no pork flavor. Leaf lard has been my fat of choice ever since I learned to render it when I was a little girl on the Missouri hog farm of my grandparents.*

*The dough can be frozen for up to 3 months. Wrap each disc tightly in two layers of plastic wrap.*

1. Refrigerate a large mixing bowl for 15 minutes to get it cold. Whisk together the flour, vanilla sugar, salt, and cayenne in the cold mixing bowl.

2. Add the cold butter and lard to the flour mixture; do not mix.

3. Submerge your hands in a bowl of ice water or put them under very cold running water for as long as you can stand it.

4. Using your fingertips, quickly work the butter and lard into the flour mixture.

5. Mix until the flour mixture has slightly larger than pea-sized chunks of butter still visible.

6. Add 4 tablespoons of the ice water to the flour mixture and mix together with your hands. Continue to add ice water as needed, 1 tablespoon at a time, until a very loose ball is formed. The dough will still be crumbly, but should hold together when pressed together in the palms of your hands.

7. Turn the dough out onto a cold work surface and lightly pack it together. Never . . . ever . . . ever knead the dough.

8. Divide the dough into two equal pieces (one slightly larger than the other) and form each into a disc. Cover with plastic wrap and refrigerate for 2 hours. Make sure to remove the dough from the refrigerator 10 minutes before using or it will be a pain to roll out.

9. Following the directions in the individual recipe, lightly flour your work surface and roll out the dough. You'll see beautiful chunks of butter all through the dough.

# Post-Coital Pie

### (dangerously decadent chocolate pie)

#### serves 8

Closeness.
A wrinkled broadcloth shirt, modest bare legs,
crumpled hair, two forks and two smiles.
Love.

½ recipe The Cold Truth Pie Dough (page 128)

½ cup (1 stick) butter, melted

1 cup sugar

4 tablespoons good-quality cocoa powder

2 large eggs, at room temperature

1 teaspoon vanilla paste

4 tablespoons all-purpose flour

2 ounces dark chocolate, melted and slightly cooled

Marshmallow Frosting (page 206),
prepared after the pie has cooled

❶ Preheat the oven to 375° F.

❷ On a lightly floured work surface, roll out the dough to a 12- to 13-inch round, ⅛ inch thick. Transfer the dough to a 9-inch tart pan with removable bottom and trim the edges. Freeze the crust for 10 minutes, or until firm.

❸ Line the crust with enough foil to cover the bottom and come up the sides, and top the foil with dried beans or pennies to weigh down the dough. Bake for 20 minutes, or until the sides are set. Do not turn the oven off.

❹ Remove the foil and weights. Prick the bottom of the tart with the tines of a fork, return to the oven, and bake for another 15 minutes, or until the dough is light golden. Remove from the oven and let cool while preparing the filling.

❺ In the bowl of a standing mixer fitted with the whisk attachment, beat the butter and sugar together for about 3 minutes, until the mixture is light in color. Add the cocoa powder and continue to beat until incorporated. Add the eggs one at a time and beat just until each addition is incorporated. Add the vanilla paste and beat until combined. Add the flour and beat just until mixed in. Remove the bowl from the mixer and stir the chocolate in by hand. Spoon the chocolate mixture into the pie crust.

❻ Bake for 18 minutes (the filling will be jiggly in the center but firm around the edges). Let cool until firm.

❼ Preheat the oven to broil.

❽ Top the pie with big dollops of the marshmallow frosting pulled to high peaks and place the pie under the broiler for 1 minute, or just until the tips start to brown. Serve immediately. ✳

# Fig & Pig Pies for One

### (spiced mashed figs, flaky crust, + salty prosciutto)

serves 8

From late summer through early fall across the southern United States, Brown Turkey figs are like tiny specs of glitter—you just can't get rid of them.

With only one eight-foot tree in your backyard, you would have enough figs to feed at least four families on your block. The trick is to find quick and easy ways to use the honey-ripe figs before they spoil. This dessert recipe is one of my favorites. It's fast, it's French-inspired, and it's Southerner-approved.

**4 slices prosciutto, cut or torn in half (8 pieces total)**

**½ teaspoon ground cinnamon**

**1 recipe The Cold Truth Pie Dough (page 128)**

**1 ½ pounds fresh ripe figs (I use Brown Turkey or Black Mission Figs)**

**½ teaspoon grated orange zest**

**Pinch of ground cardamom**

**6 tablespoons confectioners' sugar**

*I've found that freezing whole figs using the same method as for berries works great. First freeze them in a single layer on a baking sheet overnight, then transfer them to a zip-top bag and freeze. When you allow them to thaw, they won't be as firm as they had been before freezing, but they'll still taste great.*

*After frozen figs are thawed, remove the stems and mash with the skins on. Or peel with a paring knife and mash the figs before freezing. Allow them to thaw, drain off any excess liquid, and mix in your favorite spices.*

❶ Preheat the oven to 375° F. Line a baking sheet with parchment paper.

❷ Arrange the prosciutto pieces flat on the prepared baking sheet and sprinkle ¼ teaspoon of the cinnamon over all the pieces. Bake for 8 to 10 minutes, until crisp. Resist eating and set aside on a plate. Leave the parchment on the baking sheet.

❸ Lower the oven temperature to 350° F.

❹ On a lightly floured surface, roll out the dough to ¼ inch thick. Using a 4-inch round cutter, cut out eight rounds (you may need to re-roll the scraps to get all eight). Roll out each dough round into a thinner, larger round about ⅛ inch thick (the rounds don't need to be perfect; this is a quick rustic dessert). Place the dough rounds on the baking sheet and prick each with a fork. Bake for 15 minutes, or until they are just starting to brown. Remove from oven and let cool on the pan.

❺ Remove the stems from the figs and, if you'd like, peel using a paring knife (I peel them, but you don't have to). Mash them in a mixing bowl using a fork. Stir in the orange zest, the remaining ¼ teaspoon cinnamon, the cardamom, and 4 tablespoons of the confectioners' sugar. Divide the fig mixture evenly among the baked dough rounds, placing a scoop in the middle of each round. Spread the fig mixture, leaving a small border around the edge. Sift 1 tablespoon of the remaining confectioners' sugar over the rounds and bake for 5 minutes. Remove from the oven and let them cool for a minute.

❻ Top each fig pie with a piece of the crisp prosciutto and sift the remaining 1 tablespoon confectioners' sugar over all. Serve warm. ✷

\*

# Angry Bird Hand Pies
## (buffalo chicken pasties)
### yields 6

In Key West, Florida (a town Hemingway called home), gangs of angry feral roosters roam through seedy back alleys, across rocky beaches, and into loud bars. They own Key West and they know it. No matter what their folly, this band of bird brothers is protected by the laws of the city that make it illegal to kill a chicken. Acting on some screwy inner clock, they begin crowing not at sunrise but as early as two A.M. This is just one example of their ability to flip the bird to all who would question their freedom and authority.

On a recent trip to this southernmost tip of the United States, I happened to be sitting in a cafe on Duval Street (the epicenter of Key Weird) and glanced out the window to see a band of red-feathered bloods doing battle against two black-feathered freeloaders who were trying to steal a bite or two of their street food. Ignoring my dining companions, I watched for ten minutes as these angry birds battled for dining rights to three buffalo chicken wings lying on a paper plate in the road. The black-feathered roosters took a full-frontal approach to the food, but each time they attempted an advance, the red-feathered bloods jockeyed them out of position—a sloppy kind of chicken dance.

Two nights after being front row to the roosters' epic battle, I had a dream that I was sitting in a life-sized nest, wearing couture and eating a spicy, buttery chicken hand pie. (True story. I couldn't make this stuff up. I'm not that clever.)

Moral of the story:
Cocks really do make dreams come true.

1 pound boneless skinless chicken breasts (about 2)

Salt and freshly ground black pepper

About 2 cups chicken stock

1 bay leaf

½ cup (1 stick) butter

½ cup hot sauce (I use Pete's)

1 tablespoon vinegar

¼ teaspoon ground cayenne

½ teaspoon Worcestershire sauce

2 garlic cloves, minced

½ recipe The Cold Truth Pie Dough (page 128)

2 cups shredded mozzarella cheese

1 large egg, beaten with 1 tablespoon water

❶ Line a baking sheet with parchment paper and set aside.

❷ Generously season the chicken breasts with salt and pepper and arrange them flat in a medium saucepan. Pour in enough stock to cover the chicken by ½ inch (add more than 2 cups if necessary) and add the bay leaf. Bring the stock to a boil over high heat, then reduce the heat to low so the stock is just simmering. Cover and simmer for 10 minutes. Remove from the heat and let the chicken breasts cool, covered, in the poaching liquid for 20 minutes. When cool enough to handle, remove the breasts and use your hands to shred the chicken. Set aside. Discard the stock (and a bay leaf) or use for another pie.

❸ In a medium saucepan over low heat, melt the butter. Whisk in the hot sauce, vinegar, cayenne, Worcestershire sauce, and garlic and simmer for 5 minutes. Season with salt and pepper to taste. Remove from the heat and add the chicken. Toss to coat. Set aside.

❹ Preheat the oven to 375° F.

❺ On a lightly floured surface, divide the dough into six equal pieces and roll each out into an 8-by-4-inch rectangle (give or take; these don't need to be perfect), ⅛ to ¼ inch thick. Using 1 cup of the cheese divided into six portions, spread the cheese onto the lower half of each rectangle (making sure to leave a ½-inch border around the edge). Divide the shredded chicken mixture evenly among the six hand pies by piling it on top of the cheese. Sprinkle the remaining 1 cup cheese evenly over the chicken mounds. Brush the edges of the dough with the egg mixture and fold the top half of the dough over the filling,

aligning the sides. Press the edges together and seal with the tines of a fork. No need to get fancy here—these birds are mad. Place the hand pies on the prepared baking sheet and brush the tops of each hand pie lightly with the remaining egg mixture.

❻ Bake the hand pies for 20 minutes, or until golden brown. Let cool for 10 minutes before serving. Always, always eat them warm—always—unless, of course, you want to eat them cold. ✻

# Wascally Wabbit Pot Pie

### (rich rabbit confit, woodsy vegetables, flaky pastry)

serves 6

I've been eating rabbit since I was a young girl. Squirrel, too, for that matter, but my husband begs me not to mention that in the company of his peers.

It was only in the past few years that I learned that rabbit meat is low in saturated fat, cholesterol, and calories, and is also an excellent source of B-12 and niacin. As one of the most productive of all livestock, rabbits can gain up to five pounds more meat on the same feed and water than one cow can.

If you aren't familiar with rabbit, I beg you to give this meat a try. Ask at your local farmers' market—you can usually find it there or in the freezer section of most upscale grocery stores. If not, just use chicken. But never squirrel. Never.

**For the rabbit confit:**

3 garlic cloves, minced

2 teaspoons freshly ground black pepper

1 teaspoon fresh thyme leaves

1 teaspoon finely chopped fresh rosemary

1 tablespoon finely chopped fresh parsley

2 tablespoons salt

About 2 cups vegetable oil, lard, or duck fat

1 rabbit, dressed, butchered, and cleaned (about 3 pounds)

**For the pie:**

5 tablespoons butter

1 cup sliced fingerling potatoes

Salt

2 large carrots, peeled and thinly sliced

1 small leek (white part only), cleaned and thinly sliced

1 garlic clove, minced

1 teaspoon fresh thyme leaves

2 stalks celery, roughly chopped

3 tablespoons all-purpose flour

3 to 4 cups warm chicken stock or vegetable stock

1 cup sliced button mushrooms

1 tablespoon chopped fresh parsley

Freshly ground black pepper

1 recipe The Cold Truth Pie Dough (page 128)

1 large egg, beaten

*The filling recipe for my pot pie is one I use with many different types of meats. You may be thinking, Where are the peas and corn, Libbie? Here's the thing: I don't like peas and corn in my pot pies. If you do, then add them. Also, if you don't feel up to trying your hand at rabbit confit, try using 2 pounds shredded poached chicken thighs or turkey, or even leftover fried chicken, crust and all!*

may need to add more oil to make sure the rabbit pieces are completely covered) and continue to bake for 1 hour more, or until the meat is tender. Remove from the oven and let the rabbit cool in the oil. (The confit can be stored with the pieces submerged in the fat in the same cooking pot in the refrigerator for several weeks.)

❹ The meat should fall off the bones. When ready to use, remove the meat from the bones and shred with your fingers.

❺ **Make the pie:** Grease the inside of a 2-quart casserole dish with 1 tablespoon of the butter and set aside.

❻ Put the potatoes in a saucepan and cover with cold water by 1 inch. Bring to a boil, uncovered, and cook for 3 to 4 minutes, until crisp-tender. Drain and set aside.

❼ Bring a medium saucepan of water and 1 teaspoon salt to a boil. Add the carrots and cook for about 3 minutes, until crisp-tender. Drain and set aside.

❽ In a large heavy saucepan over medium heat, combine the remaining 4 tablespoons butter, the leek, garlic, thyme, and celery. Cook, stirring constantly, for 5 minutes, or until the celery is cooked through. Still over medium heat, stir in the flour until all the vegetables are coated. Gradually stir in the stock and cook for about 4 minutes, until thickened. Add the mushrooms, parsley, carrots, potatoes, and confit and stir until combined. Pour the mixture into the prepared casserole dish and set aside.

❾ Preheat the oven to 400° F.

❿ Roll out the dough to a 10-inch round, ¼ inch thick, that is 1-inch larger than your dish. Cut a small hole in the center of the dough to allow the steam to escape. Center the hole over the casserole dish and drape the dough so that it covers the entire dish. Using kitchen shears, trim the edges to a ½-inch overhang. Turn the edges under and decoratively crimp the sides to seal the dough to the casserole dish. You can also leave the overhang the way it is, but make sure to seal the edges by pressing your fingers around the top of the casserole dish. Brush the dough with the egg and place the casserole on a baking sheet. Bake for 45 minutes, or until the crust is a rich golden brown and the filling is bubbly. Serve hot. ✳

❶ **Make the rabbit confit:** Stir together the garlic, pepper, thyme, rosemary, parsley, and salt in a small mixing bowl. Rub the mixture over all the rabbit pieces and refrigerate, covered, overnight.

❷ Preheat the oven to 300° F.

❸ Heat the fat in a Dutch oven over medium heat until it just begins to shimmer (do not boil). Add the rabbit pieces and turn to completely coat them in the oil. Add enough oil to the pot to completely cover the rabbit pieces by ½ inch. Still over medium heat, bring the oil to just the shimmering stage (do not allow to boil), then cover the pot and transfer it to the oven. Bake for 1 hour. Turn the pieces over in the oil (at this point, you

\*

# Stoned Tart

### (rum, stone fruits, + pistachio cream)

serves 8

I used to think that people who made tarts only did so because they weren't equipped to make the real deal: a pie. In my small mind, the product of what I thought was a bourgeois upbringing, tarts were a sort of steerage-class dessert, a recipe you reached for only if you were an amateur, blazed, or just plain lazy. After all, you must be affected in some way if you didn't put another layer of flaky dough over that fruit filling, am I right?

My ridiculous tart bigotry was put to the test when, in my twenties, I worked for a militant Swiss chef. This six-foot-six-inch giant of a man, with his blindingly shiny shoes and perfect blond comb-over, was the first person since my mother to bring me to tears in a kitchen. The day I had the arrogance to question one of his tart recipes will forever be marked in my mind as the day Switzerland gave up its neutrality.

Chef went mad-cow crazy. Pots, pans, and colorful language all flew in my direction. When you hear the phrase "insolent little puke" screamed at you in a Swiss-German accent, from an inch in front of your face, you will never forget it.

It was also, as I now remember, the first day of my love affair with tarts.

¾ cup all-purpose flour

2 tablespoons yellow cornmeal

¼ cup plus 2 teaspoons vanilla sugar (page 202)

4 tablespoons cold butter, cubed

2 to 4 tablespoons ice water

¾ cup shelled pistachios

¼ cup heavy cream

½ teaspoon S&V House Blend Almond Extract (page 199)

5 stone fruits (any mixture of apricots, peaches, nectarines, or plums), pitted and sliced, skins on

2 tablespoons dark brown sugar

2 teaspoons fresh lemon juice

1 tablespoon Gosling's Black Seal rum

½ teaspoon S&V House Blend Citrus Extract (page 199)

¼ teaspoon ground cinnamon

Pinch of salt

Ice cream or whipped cream, for serving (optional)

❶ In a medium mixing bowl, whisk together the flour, cornmeal, and ¼ cup vanilla sugar. Cut in the butter using your fingers or two knives. Add 2 tablespoons ice water to the dough and stir to combine. Continue to add ice water by the tablespoon until the dough comes together (this should take no more than 4 tablespoons). Turn the dough out onto a piece of plastic wrap, wrap well, and refrigerate for 30 minutes.

❷ In a food processor with the blade attachment, pulse the pistachios until roughly chopped. Add the remaining 2 teaspoons vanilla sugar, heavy cream, and almond extract. Pulse until a thick paste forms. Set aside.

❸ In a large mixing bowl, stir the fruit slices together with the brown sugar, lemon juice, rum, citrus extract, cinnamon, and salt.

❹ Spray a 9 ½-inch round, 9-inch square, or 13 ¾-inch rectangular tartpan with removable bottom with nonstick baking spray. Remove the dough from the refrigerator and unwrap it. On a lightly floured work surface, roll out the dough to ¼- inch thick. Drape and press the dough into the prepared pan, covering the bottom and sides, with some overhang.

❺ Roll a rolling pin over the edges of the tart pan to cleanly cut off the excess dough. Spread the pistachio mixture over the bottom of the dough and arrange the fruit slices on top. Refrigerate to firm up the dough while the oven is preheating.

❻ Preheat the oven to 400° F. Line a baking sheet with foil.

❼ Transfer the tart from the refrigerator to the baking sheet and bake in the lower third of the oven for 40 to 50 minutes, until the fruit begins to bubble. Remove from the oven and let cool completely on a wire rack before slicing. Serve with ice cream or whipped cream. ✳

show & tell

# Guerilla Pie Decorating

## (creative crimping)

The secret to creative pie decorating? Think outside your thumbs.

*Make sure to wipe off your pearls before and after crimping, using a soft cloth that has been lightly dampened with a mild soap and water. To my embarrassment, I once made the mistake of forgetting to clean mine before wearing them to a cocktail party. Imagine my horror when a certain University of Georgia Tri-Delta host asked me what kind of pearls I was wearing. Apparently, she had never seen such a "crusty" variety before.*

**1  Cork Screw Crimping**

For a 9-inch pie, roll out your top pie dough to an 11-inch round, ⅛ inch thick. Drape the dough over the pie plate and turn the overhang under to create a thicker rim around the pie. Use an open corkscrew to decoratively crimp the edges (then open a bottle of wine to enjoy while your pie is baking).

**2  Measuring Spoon Crimping**

For a 9-inch pie, roll out your top pie dough to an 11-inch round, ⅛ inch thick. Drape the dough over the pie plate and turn the overhang under to create a thicker rim around the pie. Turn a ½-teaspoon measure upside down to decoratively crimp the rim. Let the circles intersect for an arty look.

**3  Strand of Pearls Crimping**

For a 9-inch pie, roll out your top pie dough to an 11-inch round, ⅛ inch thick. Drape the dough over the pie plate and turn the overhang under to create a thicker rim around the pie. Using a strand of oversized pearls, push them into the rim of the pie and pull away to reveal the magic.

**4  Tong Crimping**

For a 9-inch pie plate, roll out your pie dough to a 12-inch circle that is ⅛-inch thick. Drape the dough over the pie plate and turn the overhang under to create a thicker rim around the pie. Use the tip of a pair of tongs to pinch a decorative pattern around the edge.

*continued on page 142*

show & tell

## Guerilla Pie Decorating, continued

**⑤ Covering in Cutouts**

Using the pie dough recipe for a double-crust pie (page 128), roll out the first disc to a 12-inch round, ⅛ inch thick. Drape it into a 9-inch pie plate and allow the overhang to extend over the edge. Pile in the pie filling and dot the top with butter. Fold the overhanging dough up onto the filling. Roll out the second disc to ⅛ inch thick and cut out whatever shape you choose—I've used a maple leaf cutter here (no Canadian chauvinism from me). From the edge of the pie, work around and inward, overlapping the cutouts to form the top crust and using a simple egg wash as a glue (1 egg yolk, beaten with 1 tablespoon milk or water). Keep adding cutouts until the entire pie is covered in dough. Be sure to leave a few small open areas, or a hole in the top, to let the steam escape.

**⑥ Kilroy Was Here Crimping**

For a 9-inch pie, roll out your pie dough to an 11-inch round, ⅛ inch thick. Drape the dough into the pie plate and trim away any overhang. Crimp the edge of the pie in a traditional way, pinching with the thumb and forefinger of one hand on the outside of the dough and pushing the forefinger of your other hand into the pinched area. Roll the dough scraps into balls and pinch the front to shape a nose. Use a simple egg wash (1 egg, beaten with 1 tablespoon water) to glue the heads into the "divots" of the crimping. Kids love this one. It bakes up creepy cool, and you can teach them about graffiti art from the 1940s, when Kilroy originated. I like to think of it as an educational crimp.

# Preggers Pink Pickle Pie

## (a sweet + sour craving pie)

serves 8

I live in what must be the most fertile neighborhood in Savannah, Georgia. In the past five years, since my husband and I moved in, I know, by name, ten babies that have been born on our block. There is an eleventh and twelfth, but for the life of me I can't remember their names. If I squint my eyes and concentrate hard enough I'm pretty sure they both start with a hard C, but I wouldn't bet my dog on it. I'll wait to ask when they're old enough to spell it.

On this street (which has been compared to the set of *The Truman Show*), I've become a keen observer of the pregnant women in my midst. I pretend to listen as they talk their foreign language of "what to expect when they least expect it," or something along those lines. And I actually listen when they talk about the crazy things they put in their mouths for fetal sustenance—a subject that never fails to fascinate me.

My favorite preggers neighbor, Margaret, once frightened the other gorilla mothers by telling them her lunch consisted of a fat dill pickle and a slice of pie, washed down with a tumbler of cherry Kool-Aid. This didn't disturb me at all. The sweet-and-sour flavor combination reminded me of cherry Kool-Aid pickles sold at roadside markets in the Deep South, and got me thinking about how good a pickle pie could be.

I dedicate this recipe to all the mothers out there. If the math continues the way it has, there will be another couple neighborhood babies born by the time this book is published. Don't count on me to remember their names.

---

½ recipe The Cold Truth Pie Dough (page 128)

3 large eggs

½ cup sugar

½ teaspoon lemon extract (page 199)

½ teaspoon ground cinnamon

¼ teaspoon freshly grated nutmeg

1 tablespoon cornstarch

½ cup heavy cream

2 tablespoons butter, melted

1 cup drained and finely ground Red Kool-Aid Pickles (recipe follows; use a food processor or box grater to grind them)

Whipped cream, for garnish (optional)

❶ Preheat the oven to 350° F.

❷ On a lightly floured work surface, roll out the larger disc of dough to a 12-inch round, about ⅛ inch thick. Gently drape the dough into a 9-inch pie pan. (Draping is the key: You don't want to push the pie dough into the pan; just let it fall naturally). Trim the dough to create a 1-inch overhang from the edge of the pie pan. (Kitchen shears are the best tool for this.) Turn the overhang under and decoratively crimp the edges (see "Guerilla Pie Decorating," page 140 for a bunch of fun crimping ideas). Refrigerate until ready to use.

❸ In the bowl of a standing mixer fitted with the whisk attachment, whisk the eggs and sugar. Beat on medium speed for 3 minutes, until thick and light yellow in color. Reduce the speed to low and add the lemon extract, cinnamon, nutmeg, cornstarch, heavy cream, and butter. Beat until well combined. Fold in the pickles. Pour the mixture into the chilled pie shell and bake for 45 to 60 minutes, until set (the filling will be jiggly in the center but firm around the edges). Let cool on a wire rack before serving. Garnish with whipped cream, if you like. I like. ✳

### Red Kool-Aid Pickles
yields 1 (90-ounce) jar

Sweet-and-sour pickles you can eat whole—just be aware that your fingers will turn the color of the pickle.

1 (90-ounce) jar of whole dill pickles

4 packets Kool-Aid (I prefer cherry—it's just how I roll)

2 cups sugar

Drain the juice from the pickle jar and discard, leaving the pickles inside.

In a medium pitcher, combine the Kool-Aid, sugar, and 4 cups water. Stir until the sugar is completely dissolved. Pour enough of the Kool-Aid mixture over the pickles in the jar to completely cover them. Put the lid on the jar and refrigerate for 1 to 2 weeks before eating. *

*Question: Why do pregnant women always cup their bellies when photographed? I remember being pregnant, but I don't remember belly-cupping every time a camera was pointed at my baby bump. The pose puzzles me, but I've learned to accept it. After all, who am I to say that a baby wouldn't fall out if it weren't held up from the outside. I'm not a doctor . . . just a pie maker.*

✳

# Sweet & Sour Cherry Pie

### (an uncommon cherry pie)

**serves 8**

There are only two things I consider sacrilegious:

1. Anyone but Steve Perry fronting the band Journey.
2. Cherry pie from a can.

I'm resolved that I can't do anything about Journey's current lineup, but I can do something about the pie—and here it is. A sweet-and-sour pie. The most uncommon cherry pie you will ever eat. "Don't stop believin'."

6 cups fresh or frozen sour cherries, pitted

1 ⅓ cups sugar

4 tablespoons instant tapioca, pulverized to a fine powder (use a zip-top bag and a rolling pin to crush)

1 tablespoon balsamic vinegar

½ teaspoon S&V House Blend Almond Extract (page 199)

1 recipe The Cold Truth Pie Dough (page 128)

2 tablespoons cold unsalted butter, cubed

1 egg, beaten with 1 tablespoon water or milk

Vanilla ice cream

4 tablespoons prepared balsamic glaze (see Note)

❶ In a large mixing bowl, stir together the cherries, sugar, and tapioca powder. Fold in the vinegar and almond extract. Set aside.

❷ On a lightly floured work surface, roll out the larger disc of dough to a 12-inch round, about ⅛ inch thick. Gently drape the dough into a 9-inch pie pan. (Draping is the key: You don't want to push the pie dough into the pan; just let it fall naturally). Trim the dough to create a ½-inch overhang from the edge of the pie pan. (Kitchen shears are the best tool for this.) Fill the pie shell with the cherry filling and dot the top with the cubed butter. Roll the remaining dough out to an 11-inch round, about ⅛ inch thick. If you wish to do so, make any decorative cutouts to the dough at this point. Center and drape the dough over the pie. Tuck the top crust under the bottom crust and crimp the two together in a decorative way (see "Guerilla Pie Decorating," page 140). At this point, you can use any dough scraps to decorate the top of your pie. Use the egg mixture as glue to adhere the cutouts to the top crust. Just make sure you have at least one hole in the top of the pie to allow steam to escape.

❸ Refrigerate the pie while the oven is preheating.

❹ Preheat the oven to 400° F and position an oven rack in the lower third of the oven.

❺ Line a baking sheet with foil.

❻ Place the chilled pie on the baking sheet and brush the top of the pie with the remaining egg mixture. Bake for 15 minutes, then reduce the oven temperature to 350° F and continue to bake for 45 to 60 minutes, until the filling is bubbling and the crust is golden brown. If the crust starts to turn too brown before the pie is fully baked, cover the pie loosely with foil. Let cool completely on a wire rack. Slice and serve with a scoop of vanilla ice cream and a drizzle of balsamic glaze. ✳

*Balsamic glaze can be found at supermarkets in the vinegar and oil section.*

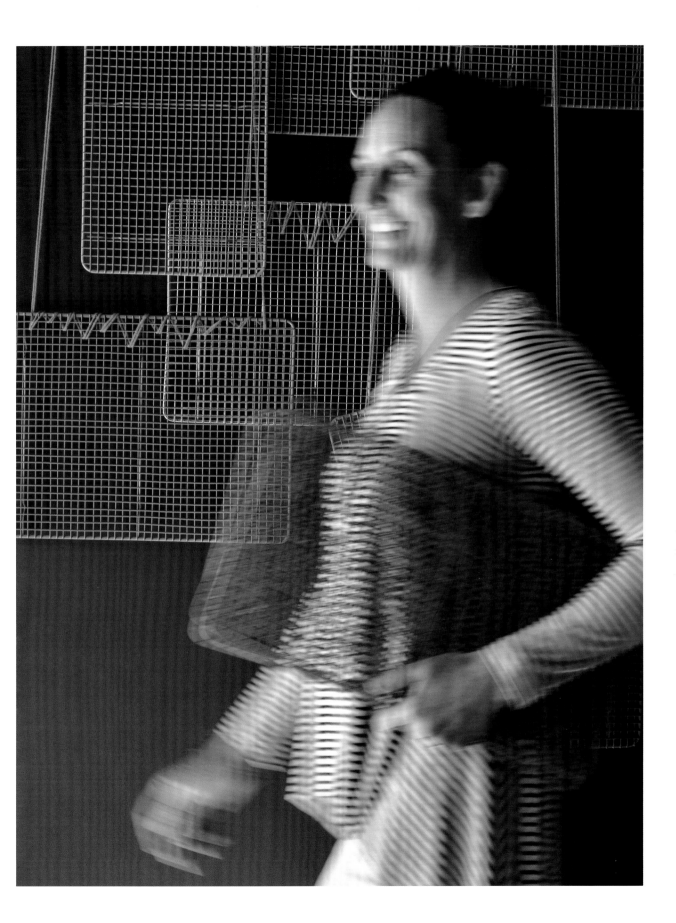

# Green Tomato Pie

### (tart + flaky with just a little sweet heat)

serves 8

¾ cup granulated sugar

½ teaspoon ground cinnamon

¼ teaspoon freshly grated nutmeg

¼ teaspoon ground cayenne

2 tablespoons all-purpose flour

1 recipe The Cold Truth Pie Dough (page 128)

2 pounds green tomatoes, cored and thinly sliced (⅛- to 1⁄16-inch thick)

¼ cup apple cider vinegar

4 tablespoons butter, cubed

1 egg, beaten with 1 tablespoon water

1 tablespoon turbinado sugar

**❶** In a small mixing bowl, stir together the granulated sugar, cinnamon, nutmeg, cayenne, and flour. Set aside.

**❷** On a lightly floured work surface, roll out the larger disc of dough to a 12-inch round, about ⅛ inch thick. Gently drape the dough into a 9-inch pie pan. (Draping is the key: You don't want to push the pie dough into the pan; just let it fall naturally). Trim the dough to create a ½-inch overhang from the edge of the pie pan. (Kitchen shears are the best tool for this.)

**❸** Arrange a layer of the tomatoes in the bottom of the pie shell. Sprinkle the tomatoes with some of the flour mixture. Repeat the layers until all of the tomatoes and flour mixture have been used. Sprinkle the vinegar over the top and dot with the butter.

**❹** Roll out the remaining dough to an 11-inch round, about ⅛ inch thick. Make decorative cut-outs with cookie cutters so steam can escape from the pie as it bakes. Center and drape the dough over the pie. Tuck the edges of the top crust under the bottom crust and crimp together in a decorative way (see "Guerilla Pie Decorating," page 140).

**❺** At this point, you can use any dough scraps to decorate the top of your pie. You are only limited by the scraps you have. Use some of the egg mixture as glue to adhere the dough scraps to the top crust. Make sure you have at least one hole in the top of the pie to allow steam to escape. Refrigerate the pie for 30 minutes.

**❻** Position an oven rack in the lower third of the oven and preheat the oven to 425° F. Line a baking sheet with foil.

**❼** Place the chilled pie on the baking sheet, brush the top of the pie with the egg mixture, and sprinkle with the turbinado sugar. Bake for 20 minutes. Reduce the oven temperature to 375° F and continue baking for 40 minutes, or until the filling is bubbling and the crust is golden brown. If the crust starts getting too brown before the pie is fully baked, cover loosely with foil. Remove from the oven and let cool completely on a wire rack before serving. ✳

# Like babies and Southern belles, not all pies are made to be entirely sweet.

# Wahini Pie

## (macadamia nut pie)

serves 8

*Wahini* is the Hawaiian word for woman or queen. In my small world, woman and queen are interchangeable. Luckily, in my husband's world they are as well. This salty, sweet pie is fit for any queen. It's my go-to pie for the holidays, and no one has ever been disappointed that there wasn't a pecan pie on the table.

½ recipe The Cold Truth Pie Dough (page 128)

3 large eggs

½ cup vanilla sugar (page 202)

1 cup light corn syrup (must be light; don't even think about using dark)

2 teaspoons vanilla extract (page 198)

2 cups salted macadamia nuts, roughly chopped

3 tablespoons butter, melted

Whipped cream (optional)

❶ Preheat the oven to 325° F. Line a baking sheet with foil.

❷ On a lightly floured work surface, roll the dough out to an 11-inch round, about ⅛ inch thick. Gently drape the dough into a 9-inch pie pan. (Draping is the key: You don't want to push the pie dough into the pan; just let it fall naturally). Trim the dough to create a 1-inch overhang from the edge of the pie pan. (Kitchen shears are the best tool for this.) Turn the edge of the dough under and decoratively crimp (see "Guerilla Pie Decorating," page 140). Refrigerate while you make the filling.

❸ In a medium mixing bowl, whisk together the eggs, vanilla sugar, corn syrup, and vanilla extract. Stir in the nuts and melted butter. Transfer the pie shell from the refrigerator to the baking sheet. Give the filling another good stir and gently pour it into the pie shell. Bake for 50 to 60 minutes, until set (the filling will be jiggly in the center but firm around the edges). Let cool completely on a wire rack.

❹ When cool, place in the refrigerator to chill—this will firm up the pie. Before serving, let stand at room temperature for 30 minutes. Serve with whipped cream, if you like. ✳

# cookies

*I freeze cookie dough in an airtight container for up to three months, but I don't like to freeze baked cookies.
They just loose something—mainly taste. I like to store baked cookies in an airtight container
for no more than three days. They never last longer than that anyway.*

Opposite: Southern Satorialist's Cookies, page 172

✳

# Side-Slap & Tickle Cookies

## (chocolate malt crackle)

### yields 24 cookies

Paul is a former musical theater performer, a fellow native Missourian, who actually starred in *Meet Me in St. Louis* at the Muny Theater in Forest Park. If you're not currently holding a Budweiser, you may not know that's a big hairy St. Louis deal. I knew I liked Paul even before I discovered he sang and danced at the Muny—and owned jazz shoes in three different kinds of exotic leathers.

Paul is also a great home cook and a baker of sorts. I begged him to test some of my recipes for this book. Not just because I trusted his and his partner Terrence's palates, but because I selfishly dreamed of singing on stage with him. I would allow him to choreograph our number, of course, but we would have to fight for the Judy Garland role.

This cookie—one of my favorites—had a different name until Paul tested it. His notes on the recipe that came back to me said "I LOVE this cookie! It was like a side-slap and a tickle all packed into one." Paul, my Midwestern thespian friend, this cookie is for you and every ingenue who ever stood on the Muny stage.

1 ⅔ cups all-purpose flour, sifted

½ cup unsweetened dark cocoa powder

6 tablespoons malted milk powder

1 ½ teaspoons baking powder

¼ teaspoon salt

½ cup (1 stick) butter, at room temperature

1 cup granulated sugar

2 large eggs, at room temperature

½ teaspoon vanilla paste

24 malted milk balls, crushed

⅓ cup confectioners' sugar

❶ In a medium bowl, whisk together the flour, cocoa powder, 2 tablespoons of the malted milk powder, the baking powder, and salt. Set aside.

❷ In the bowl of a standing mixer fitted with the paddle attachment, cream together the butter and granulated sugar until light and fluffy. Scrape down the bowl as needed. Add the eggs one at a time, beating well after each addition. Add the vanilla paste and beat until just combined. With the mixer on low speed, gradually add the flour mixture and beat until just incorporated. Stir in the malted milk balls. Remove the bowl from the standing mixer and refrigerate for 30 minutes.

❸ Preheat the oven to 350° F. Line two baking sheets with parchment paper and set aside.

❹ In a small bowl, stir together the remaining 4 tablespoons malted milk powder and the confectioners' sugar. Use a 1-tablespoon measure to scoop the dough, then roll each portion into a ball. Repeat until all the dough has been used. Roll each dough ball in the confectioners' sugar mixture until it is uniformly coated, then place on the prepared baking sheet 2 inches apart. Bake for 8 to 10 minutes, until the cookies begin to crackle on top (they look kind of like the surface of the moon).

❺ Let the cookies cool for 15 minutes before the slapping and tickling commences. ✳

✳

# Jacked-Up Ginger Cookies
### (big flavor with twice the ginger)
#### yields 30 cookies

God, I love these cookies! Take everything that is good and holy in this world and roll it in raw sugar and minced crystallized ginger and you'll experience the magic of these Jacked-up Ginger Cookies. I can eat twenty in the middle of a crowded yoga class that's twenty days into a thirty-day "clean program"—and still feel good about myself. You will too.

2 ¼ cups all-purpose flour

3 teaspoons ground ginger

1 teaspoon baking soda

¼ teaspoon salt

¾ cup (1 ½ sticks) butter, at room temperature

1 cup packed dark or light brown sugar (either works great)

1 large egg

¼ cup molasses

1 ½ tablespoons minced fresh ginger

½ cup turbinado sugar
(I use Sugar in the Raw—just lift an extra packet each time you visit a coffee shop . . . it will take 12 visits.)

¼ cup minced crystallized ginger

❶ In a medium mixing bowl, whisk together the flour, ground ginger, baking soda, and salt and set aside.

❷ In a large bowl, use a hand mixer to cream together the butter and brown sugar until smooth. Beat in the egg and molasses. Gradually mix in the flour mixture. Mix in the fresh ginger. Cover and refrigerate the dough for at least 2 hours, or overnight. (The dough is like gingerbread on steroids. Give it a taste. Trust me.)

❸ Preheat the oven to 350° F. Line a baking sheet with parchment paper and set aside.

❹ In a small mixing bowl, stir together the turbinado sugar and crystallized ginger. Shape the dough using a small portion scoop into 1 ½-inch balls and roll the balls in the turbinado sugar mixture. Place them 2 inches apart on the prepared baking sheet and bake for 10 to 12 minutes, until lightly browned. Let cool and serve. ✳

❋

# Majorette Biscotti

### (spicy chocolate baton-length dunking cookies)

**yields 4 uber-long biscotti; serves 10 to 12 if you want to break them up (I would never)**

In my closet hangs a gold-sequined leotard and two blue furry majorette hats, yet I've never led a marching band into a football stadium. The hats make an appearance during the holiday season as I try to pass them off as some sort of Alexander McQueen–inspired nutcracker decoration. Nobody buys it. In addition to the two majorette hats and leotard, I have three twirling batons of varying weights and lengths, yet I can only twirl them using a childish figure-eight technique. I'm currently hunting for a pair of white patent-leather calf boots with a moveable tassel that will swing back and forth as I step off and march in time. When I find them, my double life will be complete. Until then, I'll bake these ridiculously good baton-length biscotti, twirl them in a figure eight, and stand in my kitchen dreaming of being a band geek.

2 cups all-purpose flour, plus more for dusting

¼ cup good-quality cocoa powder

2 teaspoons baking powder

Pinch of salt

½ teaspoon ground chipotle pepper

¼ teaspoon ground cinnamon

3 large eggs, at room temperature

¾ cup sugar

1 teaspoon vanilla paste

1 cup whole raw almonds

❶ Preheat the oven to 350° F. Line a large baking sheet with parchment paper and set aside.

❷ In a medium mixing bowl, whisk together the flour, cocoa powder, baking powder, salt, chipotle pepper, and cinnamon.

❸ In the bowl of a standing mixer fitted with the paddle attachment, beat the eggs, sugar, and vanilla paste until smooth. With the mixer on low speed, add the flour mixture and mix for 3 to 4 minutes, until fully combined. Add the almonds and stir until just combined.

❹ Turn the dough out onto a lightly floured surface and knead it a couple of times. Place the dough on the baking sheet and shape it into a long log, about 18 inches long by 4 inches wide and 1 inch thick. Bake for 30 minutes, until the biscotto is firm to the touch. Remove from the oven and transfer to a wire rack to cool completely.

❺ Using a serrated knife, slice a thin slice off both sides lengthwise, then slice the remaining dough lengthwise into 4 long slices, each ¾ inch wide. Lay the slices cut side down on the baking sheet and bake for another 25 to 30 minutes, turning once halfway through the baking time, until crisp and hard. Transfer to a wire rack to cool again completely. Twirl, eat, and dream. ✳

*For a last course of a dinner party, I serve these impressively long, spicy chocolate biscotti lying atop a piping hot cup of cafe au lait. Any leftovers my guests can take home for their next coffee-dunking experience.*

*For gift giving, I pack these biscotti in baguette bags and tie with a ribbon—sparkly, of course.*

\*

# Backhanded Compliment Cookies

### (catty fortune cookies)

#### yields 16 cookies

When talking behind someone's back just doesn't make you happy, try this delicious cookie instead.

**2 large egg whites**

**½ cup all-purpose flour, sifted**

**½ cup superfine sugar**

**1 ¼ teaspoons S&V House Blend Almond Extract (page 199)**

**Pinch of salt**

**16 backhanded compliments written on 16 (½-by-5-inch) strips of paper using a nontoxic pen (see backhanded compliment suggestions below)**

**Backhanded Compliments for Beginners:**

"That's a pretty dress. Did you make it yourself?" (Classic Southern.)

"Thanks for reposting that on Facebook. I didn't have time to read it the other ten times."

"You look so pretty, I didn't even recognize you."

"Thanks for the compliment. You're much sweeter than I thought."

"It's so great to see a woman who isn't afraid to show her age."

"You look great! I can't even tell you put on that extra weight."

"Your makeup is flawless. How many hours did it take you?"

**Advanced Backhanded Compliments:**

"You have nine cats? Wow! It only smells like four or five."

"If you weren't overweight, you'd be prettier than your brother."

"I really love listening to you. You make me feel so smart."

"Amazing! I've never seen a man put away that many wine coolers."

❶ Preheat the oven to 400° F.

❷ Line a baking sheet with a silicone mat sprayed with nonstick cooking spray and set aside. Have a standard muffin tin ready.

❸ In a large mixing bowl, whisk the egg whites until foamy. Add the flour, superfine sugar, almond extract, 2 tablespoons water, and the salt and whisk for another 30 seconds, or until smooth. Preparing two cookies at a time on the baking sheet, measure 1 tablespoon batter and pour it onto a spot in the middle of one half of the baking sheet. Use the back of the tablespoon to spread the batter out into a super-thin, 4-inch-diameter circle. Repeat this process on the other half of the baking sheet to create a second thin cookie. Bake the cookies on the middle rack of the oven for 6 to 8 minutes, until golden brown around the edges.

❹ Working quickly (the cookies begin to harden about 10 seconds after you remove them from the oven), use an offset spatula to remove the cookie from the cookie sheet and lay 1 backhanded compliment down the center of the cookie. Using your fingers, fold the cookie in half and pinch the top together to form a loose semi-circle. Hold the cookie with your index fingers inserted at each open end, and slide your thumbs together along the bottom line. Press into the center of the cookie while bending the two open ends together and down to meet and form the shape of a fortune cookie.

❺ Place the shaped cookies in the muffin tin to cool (this will help the cookie keep its shape as it cools). Repeat with the other cookie. Continue until all the batter has been used and you're feeling a little bad about yourself. Not really. \*

*My friends have a sense of humor drier than most, but trust me, there is no hostess gift more fun to give than these cookies! I have had friends call me the next day wailing with laughter. So I consider this a perfect gift—one that is delicious and entertaining.*

\*

# Cowboy Crackers

## (mini-cowboy-shaped sweet buttery cookies)

### yields about 100 cookies

Cowboys are six-string guitar players, writers of Plains-inspired poetry, masters of the two-step and calf roping. Cowboys are gentlemen. At least that's what I thought at seventeen.

I met him at the Show-Me State Fair. He'd just come off a win in his heat of barrel racing when my dirty boots and glaringly white teeth must have caught his eye. He looked like something out of a movie—dark hair under a sweat-stained Stetson, Wrangler jeans just tight enough, and eyelashes a quarter-inch shy of freakishly long. Everything I loved in a boy—a cowboy. We small-talked an hour or so through the metal rodeo ring fence and although I never heard a "shucks, ma'am" (or actually anything I could repeat in church), I just knew he was nice. "He's just nervous around me" is what I wrote in my journal that night.

My cowboy caller showed up at my doorstep two nights later to pick me up for our date. With my six-foot-four-inch father looking over my shoulder, I closed my eyes and opened the door just knowing he'd be carrying a heart-shaped box of chocolates in one hand and a mason jar filled with wildflowers in the other. I was greeted with neither, just the same cowboy I met two nights prior—literally. He was still in the same shirt, same hat, and the same Wrangler jeans, although they were a little bit looser and dirtier now. He smelled of canned Busch beer, stale cigarettes, and, if I'm completely honest with myself, someone else's Loves Baby Soft perfume, bloodshot eyes, two days of beard growth, and a hickey he didn't even try to cover up with his colorful bandana.

I was allowed to leave the house long enough to walk him back to the car he parked in our driveway. In that short walk, he attempted things that are illegal to do with young girls, even in Missouri. I slammed his car door loud enough to wake the neighbors, flipped him the bird, and road my own high horse back to the house.

That cowboy may have had eyelashes I still think about today and he may have had know-how about breeding livestock, but he didn't come from any kind of good breeding himself. My first cowboy crush was a cad.

These life-size cookies were created in his honor.

P.S. By my eighteenth birthday, I had learned that barrel racing was actually a chick's sport.

*continued on page 164*

*Cowboy Crackers are the adult version of animal crackers, but kids will love them too! Place cowboy crackers in a jar and tie a colorful bandana around the lid for a cute gift. It's like a little cowboy terrarium!*

## Cowboy Crackers, continued

12 tablespoons (1 ½ sticks) butter, at room temperature

1 cup sugar

1 large egg

1 teaspoon S&V House Citrus Extract (page 199) or vanilla extract (page 198, but it's not the same)

2 ½ cups all-purpose flour, plus more for dusting

1 teaspoon baking powder

½ teaspoon salt

Pinch of freshly grated nutmeg

Pinch of ground mace

❶ In the bowl of a standing mixer fitted with the paddle attachment, cream together the butter and sugar for 3 minutes, or until light and fluffy. Scrape down the bowl as needed. Add the egg and citrus extract and continue to beat for 1 minute.

❷ In a medium mixing bowl, sift together the flour, baking powder, salt, nutmeg, and mace.

❸ With the mixer on low speed, add half of the flour mixture to the butter mixture and beat until just combined. Scrape down the bowl as needed. Add the remaining flour mixture and beat for 2 minutes, or until the dough pulls cleanly away from the sides of the bowl.

❹ Turn the dough out onto a work surface lightly dusted with flour and divide it into two flattened discs of equal size. Wrap in plastic wrap and refrigerate for 2 hours. (The dough will keep, refrigerated, for up to a few days.)

❺ Line two baking sheets (small enough to fit in your refrigerator, because you'll be chilling the cookies before you bake them) with parchment paper and set aside.

❻ Remove one dough disc from the refrigerator, unwrap it, and let it stand at room temperature for 5 minutes. Tear off two large pieces of plastic wrap and place the dough between the two sheets. Roll out to ⅛ inch thick. If the dough starts to crack, it is still a little too cold, so let it come to room temperature before continuing.

❼ When you have rolled it out, remove the dough from the plastic wrap and transfer to a work surface that has been lightly dusted with flour. Lightly dust the top of the dough with flour. Dip your small (animal cracker–size) cowboy cookie cutter into flour before pressing it into the dough to cut out the shape. Place the cookies on the prepared baking sheets and continue until all the dough has been used. Re-roll dough scraps to make more cookies. Refrigerate the cut-out cookies for 30 minutes.

❽ Preheat the oven to 350° F. Bake the cookies for 15 minutes, or until they are light golden brown. Transfer the baking sheets to wire racks and let the cookies cool to room temperature. Repeat the process with the second refrigerated disk of dough. ✳

✳

# Six-Way Sugar Chewies

## (one basic dough makes six different cookies)

### yields 48 cookies

Santa got first dibs on the only sugar cookies I ever had growing up. I knew from the pictures I'd seen of him in books that Santa wore white gloves. Still, that didn't help my germ phobias. Really, how clean were those gloves, what with taking care of the reindeer and all? I was not about to let some old man I'd never met—no matter how glowing the reports about him were—touch my food. Each Christmas morning I let my sisters finish off the sugar cookies that Santa allegedly didn't touch. I was fine waiting for the extras my mom had made.

I never understood how come we had sugar cookies only once a year. Not to mention the confusion about their being for someone else—a fat man in a red suit who, truth be told, was sometimes a mediocre gift giver (case in point: the sewing machine I got as a teen). Mom said sugar cookies were time consuming, with all that cutting and decorating. She had a point. Not to mention, they didn't hold up very well either. Only a few days after Santa put his cooties on my Christmas cookies, they weren't much good anyway. So, I decided to make a sugar cookie that was crazy good, super simple, chewy, and a blank canvas for most anything you wanted to put in it. It's your call whether to leave them out for Santa. I don't.

## My Original Sugar Chewies

1 cup (2 sticks) butter, at room temperature

1 ½ cups granulated sugar

1 large egg, at room temperature

1 teaspoon S&V House Blend Almond Extract (page 199)

2 ¾ cups all-purpose flour

1 teaspoon baking soda

½ teaspoon baking powder

Pinch of salt

4 tablespoons milk

Decorative sugar sprinkles or turbinado sugar

❶ Preheat the oven to 375° F. Line a baking sheet with parchment paper and set aside.

❷ In the bowl of a standing mixer fitted with the paddle attachment, cream together the butter and granulated sugar until smooth. Beat in the egg and almond extract.

❸ In a medium bowl, whisk together the flour, baking soda, baking powder, and salt.

❹ With the standing mixer on low speed, gradually add the flour mixture to the butter mixture. Mix in 2 tablespoons of the milk, or enough to just soften the dough.

❺ Roll level tablespoons of the dough into balls and place them on the prepared baking sheet. Use the spoon to flatten the top of each ball slightly and brush on just enough milk to moisten. Sprinkle with decorative sugar sprinkles or turbinado sugar.

❻ Bake for 10 to 12 minutes, until just barely golden. Let cool on the baking tray for a couple minutes before removing to a rack to cool completely.

*continued on page 166*

## Six-Way Sugar Chewies, continued

## The other 5 ways

### ❶ Chai Chewies

Substitute ½ teaspoon vanilla extract (page 198) for the S&V House Blend Almond Extract. Whisk 1 teaspoon ground cinnamon, ½ teaspoon ground cardamom, ¼ teaspoon ground allspice, and ¼ teaspoon finely ground black pepper into the flour mixture before adding to the butter mixture. Moisten the tops of the cookies with milk and sprinkle with a simple cinnamon-sugar mixture (2 teaspoons cinnamon mixed with 4 tablespoons sugar) before baking.

### ❷ Citrus Crush Chewies

Substitute 1 teaspoon S&V House Blend Citrus Extract plus ¼ teaspoon lemon extract (both page 199) for the S&V House Blend Almond Extract. Add 2 teaspoons grated orange zest, lemon zest, or grapefruit zest (or any mixture of the three) to the butter mixture.

### ❸ Lavender Sugar Chewies

Stir 1 tablespoon crushed dried organic lavender into the flour mixture before adding to the butter mixture.

### ❹ Hemingway Chewies

Add ¹⁄₁₆ teaspoon store-bought spearmint extract, 2 tablespoons finely chopped fresh basil leaves, and 1 teaspoon grated lime zest to the butter mixture just before adding the flour mixture.

### ❺ Coconut Sugar Chewies

Substitute ½ teaspoon store-bought coconut extract for the S&V House Blend Almond Extract. Fold ½ cup toasted unsweetened coconut flakes into the flour mixture before adding to the butter mixture.

CHAI

CITRUS CRUSH

LAVENDER

HEMINGWAY

COCONUT

SUGAR

✳

# Cake Scrap Cookies

### (all cake scraps welcome)

#### yields 12 cookies

2 ½ cups firmly packed cake scraps
(mix and match any flavors, and cut up any bigger pieces)

1 large egg

½ cup (1 stick) butter, at room temperature

¼ cup sugar

½ teaspoon vanilla paste

❶ In the bowl of a standing mixer fitted with the paddle attachment, mix all the ingredients for 3 to 4 minutes, until completely combined and the dough is soft. Refrigerate for 1 hour.

❷ Preheat the oven to 350° F.

❸ Line a baking sheet with parchment paper.

❹ Scoop the dough by heaping tablespoons and place them 1 inch apart on the baking sheet. Lightly press on each mound to flatten slightly. Bake for 15 minutes. Let the cookies cool before eating; they will become more firm as they cool. ✳

# I threw away my virginity long before I threw away a cake scrap.

*Try substituting different extracts (one-to-one) for the vanilla paste to change the flavor of the cookies.*

*Save your cake scraps in a zip-top bag in the freezer until you have enough to make cookies. The cake scraps will last for up to 3 months.*

✳

# Hiker's Bravado Cookies

## (peanut butter, chocolate, + pretzel cookies)

### yields 24 cookies

I was full of naive bravado in setting a goal to hike the 2,200 miles that make up the Appalachian Trail by a certain age.

"What? You started in Maine? I would only start in Georgia."

"If I didn't have a job, I would sooo thru-hike it."

"Map? Who needs a map? I've read a book on celestial navigation."

"You carried twenty pounds of gear the entire way? I would never carry more than fifteen."

"Me, use a tent? Are you kidding? I would only use a sleepsack and reflector tarp."

"Me, afraid of bears? No; bears are afraid of me."

Truth is, of those 2,200-odd miles, I have to this point hiked 9.2 (with my husband and my dog). My extra socks weighed more than two pounds. I screamed when I saw a bear track. And I brought a new tent.

My name is Libbie Summers and, though I am an Appalachian Trail Failure, these cookies are a success. Peanut butter cookies packed with everything you crave while hiking—dark chocolate, crunchy salty pretzels, sweet fruit, and creamy butter. In fact, these cookies were the best thing about my hiking trip.

2 cups peanut butter

½ cup (1 stick) butter, at room temperature

1 cup packed brown sugar

2 large eggs

2 teaspoons vanilla paste

1 ½ teaspoons baking soda

1 cup dried cranberries

1 cup dark chocolate chips

2 cups salted pretzels (I use mini pretzels)

❶ Preheat the oven to 350° F.

❷ Line a baking sheet with parchment paper and set aside.

❸ In a large mixing bowl, combine everything except the pretzels and use a wooden spoon to mix.

❹ Put the pretzels in a medium mixing bowl and crush them with your hands (not too fine—leave some nice chunks). Scoop 1 heaping tablespoon of dough per cookie and roll the dough in the crushed pretzels, lightly pressing the pretzels into the dough.

❺ Arrange the pretzel-coated cookies on the prepared baking sheet 1 inch apart. Bake for 17 minutes, or until just firm. Let the cookies cool before packing them in your backpack and pretending to hit the trail. ✳

✱

# Movie Night Cookies
### (soft chocolate + buttery popcorn flavored cookies)
yields 24 cookies

I grew up eating from three food groups: chocolate, popcorn, and Coke. Movie night around the Patrick homestead involved my own bowl of heavily salted popcorn, half a Mr. Goodbar, and a small bottle of Coca-Cola. My parents clearly hoped for a diabetic instead of a doctor or lawyer. As an adult, on my days off from cooking fancy, healthy food and acting like I know more than I do about branzino and leafy greens, dinners alone often consist of the three food groups from my youth. These Movie Night Cookies with a gummy Coke-bottle chaser are the closest thing I can get to that childhood memory without my mom standing over me yelling for me to pull my skirt down.

1 ⅔ cups all-purpose flour, sifted

½ cup unsweetened dark cocoa powder

1 ½ teaspoons baking powder

¼ teaspoon salt

½ cup (1 stick) butter, at room temperature

1 cup granulated sugar

2 large eggs, at room temperature

½ teaspoon vanilla paste

¼ teaspoon butter flavoring (found in the extracts section of your grocery store)

1 cup buttered popcorn Jelly Belly jelly beans, plus extra just for eating while you bake these cookies

½ cup confectioners' sugar

Gummy Coke bottles (optional)

❶ Preheat the oven to 350° F.

❷ Line 2 baking sheets with parchment paper and set aside.

❸ In a medium bowl, whisk together the flour, cocoa powder, baking powder, and salt. Set aside.

❹ In the bowl of a standing mixer fitted with the paddle attachment, cream together the butter and granulated sugar until light and fluffy. Scrape down the bowl as needed. Add the eggs one at a time, beating well after each addition. Add the vanilla paste and butter flavoring and beat until just combined. With the mixer on low speed, gradually add the flour mixture and beat until just blended. Fold in the jelly beans.

❺ Scoop 1 tablespoon dough and roll it into a ball. Roll the ball in the confectioners' sugar until well covered. Place on the baking sheet about 2 inches apart. Bake for 10 to 12 minutes, or until the cookies are crackled. Let cool completely before serving, with a side of gummy Coke bottles, if you like. ✱

✳

# Southern Sartorialist's Cookies

### (a salty, smoky, bourbon-laced oatmeal cookie for dudes)

#### yields 24 cookies

Even though I've been asked to swim in the lady pond more times than I can remember (I did play semi-pro softball, after all), it's men that I love. Inspiring men. Men who can design a room, stitch a dress, paint a canvas, draw a cartoon, drive a boat, catch a fish, host a television show, or take a photo—and look good doing it.

It was my dream to bring some of these dapper men together for the first annual meeting of the Southern Sartorialists (stylish men living in the South). So I did. And they came. On a cool fall day in Savannah, eight men of all ages met under a two-hundred-year-old oak tree: Matt (artist), Josh (yachstman), Ray (professor), Jamie (TV personality), Cedric (photographer), Anthony (fisherman), and Joel and Mitch (designers). They talked politics, comic books, art, and fashion, and flew paper airplanes in between bites of these lightly sweetened Bourbon-laced oatmeal cookies.

2 cups pecans, roughly chopped

½ cup (1 stick) plus 2 tablespoons butter, at room temperature

1 cup packed light brown sugar

½ teaspoon smoked salt (I use alderwood-smoked salt)

1 ¼ cups all-purpose flour

1 teaspoon baking soda

1 teaspoon ground cinnamon

½ teaspoon freshly grated nutmeg

Pinch of freshly ground black pepper

¼ cup vegetable shortening

1 teaspoon vanilla paste

¼ cup bourbon

2 tablespoons heavy cream

1 large egg, lightly beaten

1 cup old-fashioned rolled oats

❶ Preheat the oven to 350° F.

❷ Line a baking sheet with parchment paper and set aside.

❸ In a large sauté pan over medium-low heat, cook the pecans, stirring constantly, for 3 minutes, just until they begin to toast. Stir in 2 tablespoons of the butter, 1 tablespoon of the brown sugar, and the smoked salt. Remove from the heat and let cool in the pan.

❹ In a medium mixing bowl, sift together the flour, baking soda, cinnamon, nutmeg, and pepper. Set aside.

❺ In the bowl of a standing mixer fitted with the paddle attachment, beat the remaining ½ cup butter, the shortening, and the remaining brown sugar for 5 minutes, or until light and fluffy. Add the vanilla paste, bourbon, and cream and beat until well incorporated. Add the egg and beat just until combined. With the mixer on the lowest speed, slowly add the flour mixture in three increments. Remove the bowl from the standing mixer and stir in the pecan mixture and the oats by hand.

❻ Drop the dough by big heaping tablespoons onto the prepared baking sheet, spacing the cookies 2 inches apart. Bake for 12 minutes, until the cookies are puffy and lightly browned on the edges. Allow to cool on the sheet for 2 minutes, and then remove to a cooling rack. Perfect with two fingers of bourbon. ✳

No. 1
ENGLISH CLARO

\*

# Jalapeño "Sort of Shortbread" Cookies

## (an interesting shortbread cookie with a kick of heat + cooled off in chocolate)

### yields 24 cookies

I don't get shortbread; it's the Canada of cookies. It doesn't want to be the best cookie or the worst cookie—it's just happy to be somewhere in the middle. If there was a milquetoast award for food, shortbread would be in the top two—second only to actual milk and toast.

Here's where I hit a Labrador iceberg. Every. Person. I. Love. In. This. World. Loves. Shortbread.

My husband begs me to bake some for him. My best girlfriends Sydney and Brenda are the same.

"When are you baking shortbread again?"

Emmm, never?

Until now. I decided to make a "sort of shortbread" that I could pass off as the real thing. I think it's better. Kind of like a Newfoundlander or Nova Scotian, but with more shameless Saskatchewan bravado, eh?

2 cups all-purpose flour, plus more for dusting

6 tablespoons sugar

1 teaspoon baking soda

2 teaspoons cream of tartar

¼ teaspoon salt

½ cup (1 stick) cold butter, diced

2 hard-boiled egg yolks

1 teaspoon hot pepper extract (page 198)

¾ cup heavy cream

1 teaspoon finely minced jalapeño chile

6 ounces dark chocolate, coarsely chopped

❶ In the bowl of a standing mixer fitted with the paddle attachment, combine the flour, sugar, baking soda, cream of tartar, and salt. Mix for 30 seconds, until just combined. With the mixer on low speed, add the butter and mix for 2 minutes, until the mixture resembles coarse breadcrumbs. Turn off the mixer and push the egg yolks through a fine-mesh sieve into the bowl. Add the hot pepper extract, cream, and jalapeño. Mix on low speed for 3 minutes, or just until the dough comes together. Remove the dough from the bowl and form it into a flat disc. Wrap the dough in plastic wrap and refrigerate for 1 to 2 hours.

❷ Preheat the oven to 350° F. Line two baking sheets with parchment paper and set aside.

❸ On a lightly floured surface, roll out the dough to ⅛ inch thick. Cut into whatever shape you choose using a lightly floured cookie cutter. Place the cookies on the prepared baking sheet 1-inch apart and refrigerate for about 15 minutes (this will help firm up the dough so the cookies keep their shape while baking).

❹ Bake for 8 to 10 minutes, or until the cookies are lightly browned around the edges. Cool on a wire rack. Once the cookies are completely cool, you can dip the edges in melted chocolate.

❺ To do a "quick temper" on the chocolate, put half the chocolate in a heatproof bowl set over a saucepan of simmering water and stir until the chocolate is completely melted. Carefully remove the bowl from the heat and gradually add the remaining chocolate, stirring until completely melted and smooth. Working one cookie at a time, dip an end into the melted chocolate, allow any excess chocolate to drip off, and place on the other prepared baking sheet. Refrigerate until the chocolate is set then serve. To store, lay the cookies flat in an airtight container and keep in a cool place or the refrigerator (so the chocolate won't melt) for up to 1 week. \*

# Serious Oatmeal Cookies
### (a chewy fruity cookie for a serious oatmeal cookie lover)
yields 48 cookies

¼ cup dried cranberries

1 cup raisins

½ cup orange juice

½ cup (1 stick) butter, at room temperature

½ cup applesauce

1 cup packed dark brown sugar

¼ cup granulated sugar

2 large eggs

2 teaspoons S&V Citrus Extract (page 199)

1 ½ cups all-purpose flour

1 teaspoon salt

½ teaspoon baking soda

½ teaspoon baking powder

1 teaspoon ground cinnamon

¼ teaspoon ground ginger

¼ teaspoon freshly grated nutmeg

3 cups old-fashioned rolled oats

¼ cup chopped crystalized ginger

❶ In a small bowl, stir together the cranberries, raisins, and orange juice. Cover and refrigerate overnight. (If you think it's stupid that I asked you to soak your raisins and cranberries overnight, you can speed up the process by putting the dried fruit in a microwave-safe bowl, covering with orange juice, then microwaving on high for 1 minute, or until the mixture begins to bubble. Carefully remove the bowl from the microwave and let it stand for 10 minutes to cool. Then you can continue with this recipe and not think badly of me.)

❷ Preheat the oven to 350° F.

❸ Line a baking sheet with parchment paper and set aside.

❹ In the bowl of a standing mixer fitted with the paddle attachment, cream together the butter, applesauce, and both sugars until light and fluffy. Add the eggs one at a time, beating well after each addition. Stir in citrus extract. Drain the cranberries and raisins, discarding the liquid, and stir them into the butter mixture.

❺ In a medium mixing bowl, whisk together the flour, salt, baking soda, baking powder, cinnamon, ginger, and nutmeg. With the mixer on low speed, add the flour mixture to the wet mixture 1 cup at a time, until fully incorporated. Scrape down the bowl as needed. Remove the bowl from the mixer and stir in the oats and ginger.

❻ Using a 2-tablespoon measure, scoop the dough onto the baking sheet, spacing the cookies 2 inches apart. Bake for 10 to 12 minutes, until light golden brown. Let cool slightly on the baking sheet before transferring to a wire rack to cool completely. ✳

※

# Kahlo Cookies
### (strangely hot Mexican chocolate cookies)
#### yields 18 (3-inch) cookies

"I used to think I was the strangest person in the world, but then I thought: There are so many people in the world, there must be someone just like me who feels bizarre and flawed in the same ways I do. I would imagine her, and imagine that she must be out there thinking of me too. Well, I hope that if you are out there and read this and know that, yes, it's true I'm here, and I'm just as strange as you."
—Frida Kahlo

8 ounces dark chocolate, chopped

¾ cup all-purpose flour

1½ teaspoons ground cinnamon

¾ teaspoon ground chipotle pepper

½ teaspoon baking powder

¼ teaspoon salt

½ cup (1 stick) butter, at room temperature

½ cup granulated sugar

¼ cup packed dark brown sugar

2 large eggs, at room temperature

1 teaspoon vanilla paste

1 teaspoon hot pepper extract (page 198; optional)

2 tablespoons turbinado sugar

❶ Preheat the oven to 375° F. Line a baking sheet with parchment paper and set aside.

❷ Melt the chocolate in a double boiler and set aside.

❸ In a small mixing bowl, whisk together the flour, cinnamon, chipotle pepper, baking powder, and salt. Set aside.

❹ In a medium mixing bowl using a hand mixer (or in the bowl of a standing mixer fitted with the paddle attachment) on medium speed, cream together the butter, granulated sugar, and brown sugar until light and fluffy, about 5 minutes. Add the chocolate and mix on medium speed for 2 minutes. Add the eggs one at a time and mix until incorporated. Add the vanilla paste and hot pepper extract and mix until incorporated. With the mixer on low speed, gradually add the flour mixture and mix until well combined.

❺ Drop the dough by generous tablespoons 2 inches apart onto the prepared baking sheet. Sprinkle a generous amount of turbinado sugar on top of each mound of dough. Bake for 8 to 10 minutes, or just until the cookies have set. Remove from the oven and let cool completely on the baking sheet. ※

✳

# Primal Cut Cookies

## (bacon sugar cookies)

### yields 16 large hogs

Why can't a cookie be a teaching tool? Not only are these delicious, but they also demonstrate the primal cuts of a pig. The inspiration came from my *Whole Hog Cookbook*. While working on it, I realized that for pig aficionados, no meal is ever complete without a bacon dessert.

4 thin slices bacon

3 cups all-purpose flour, plus more for dusting

1 ½ teaspoons baking powder

½ teaspoon salt

¾ cup plus 2 tablespoons butter, at room temperature

1 cup sugar

1 large egg

2 ounces cream cheese

1 teaspoon S&V House Blend Citrus Extract (page 199)

1 teaspoon grated orange zest

S&V Royal Icing (page 209; optional)

❶ In a small skillet, fry the bacon until crisp. Drain on a paper towel, then chop very fine and set aside. Pour the rendered fat into a heat-resistant bowl and place in the refrigerator to cool. In a medium mixing bowl, whisk together the flour, baking powder, and salt. Set aside.

❷ In the bowl of a standing mixer fitted with the paddle attachment, beat the butter, 2 tablespoons of the cooled rendered bacon fat, and the sugar until light and fluffy (if your bacon did not render 2 tablespoons fat, use extra butter to make up the difference — you'll need 1 cup total fat). Add the egg and beat until completely combined. Add the cream cheese, citrus extract, and orange zest and beat until incorporated. Gradually beat the flour mixture into the butter mixture until completely incorporated. Add the bacon and mix until just combined. Cover the bowl with plastic wrap and refrigerate for 1 hour.

❸ Preheat the oven to 350° F. Line a baking sheet with parchment paper and set aside. Roll the dough out on a lightly floured surface to ⅛ inch thick. Using a large pig-shaped cookie cutter (template on page 180), cut out the cookies and place them on the baking sheet 1-inch apart. Bake for 8 minutes, or until the cookies are just beginning to brown. Let them cool completely on the baking sheet. If you like, decorate the cookies in a primal cut design as shown opposite.

❹ Using a pastry bag fitted with a small round #2 tip and filled with thick white icing, outline each entire cookie and then outline the pattern of the primal cuts. Using a pastry bag fitted with a small round tip (you can also use a squeeze bottle with a small opening) and filled with one color of the flood icing at a time, squeeze a small amount of the flood icing into the primal cut section you wish to color and use a toothpick to fill to the edges, if needed. Tap the cookie to help the color settle. Continue on with this color/cut/section of each cookie before changing to the next color. Continue the process until all sections are filled with color. Don't worry about everything being perfect. I've never met a pig that was. ✳

# Cookies

\*

## Primal Cut Cookie Stencil

*(recipe is on page 178)*

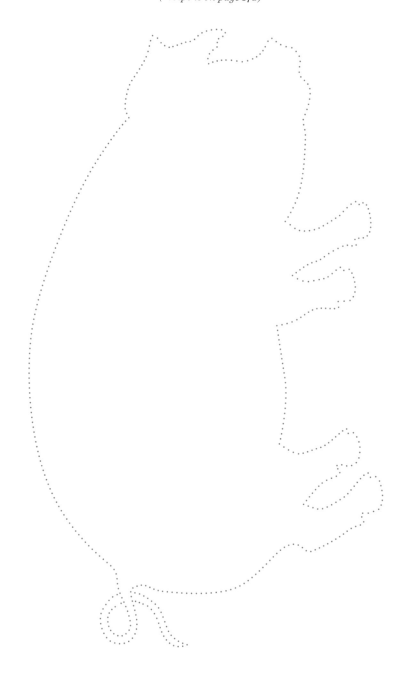

Making a custom cookie cutter is simple. Trace the shape onto a see-through paper (like tracing paper or printer paper). Cut out and trace onto a thicker surface like poster board. Cut out. Now, just place the shape onto your cookie dough and carefully cut around it with a paring knife.

# Cookies

*

## Retired Gingerbread Working Girls Cookie Stencil

*(recipe is on page 182)*

These cookies start out with a young woman's body, but quickly age as they bake.

Cookies

*

# Retired Gingerbread Working Girls

### (spicy + curvy gingerbread women)

**yields 8 to 12 cookies, depending on how far yours have let themselves go**

A bit more buxom than they were in their prime, these retired gingerbread working girls may not have seen a dance pole in years, but they still pack a dollar's worth of spice and a whole lot of fun.

3 cups all-purpose flour, plus more for dusting

¼ teaspoon salt

1 ½ teaspoons ground cinnamon

2 teaspoons ground ginger

½ teaspoon ground cloves

¼ teaspoon freshly grated nutmeg

¾ cup (1 ½ sticks) butter, at room temperature

⅔ cup packed dark brown sugar

1 large egg

½ cup molasses

½ teaspoon vanilla paste

Red Hots candies (optional)

❶ In a medium mixing bowl, whisk together the flour, salt, cinnamon, ginger, cloves, and nutmeg. Set aside.

❷ In the bowl of a standing mixer fitted with the paddle attachment, beat the butter and brown sugar until creamy. Add the egg and beat until just incorporated, then add the molasses and vanilla paste and beat for 2 minutes, or just until smooth. Gradually add the flour mixture to the butter mixture, beating until well combined. Remove the dough from the bowl, wrap it in plastic wrap, and refrigerate for 1 hour.

❸ Preheat the oven to 350° F. Line a baking sheet with parchment paper and set aside.

❹ Roll the dough out on a lightly floured surface to ⅛ inch thick. Using your favorite cookie cutters (or my stencil pattern and a paring knife), cut and place the cookies on the baking sheet about 1 inch apart. Decorate with candies at this point, if you like. (I like.)

❺ Bake for 10 minutes, or until the cookies are firm to the touch and lightly browned. Cool completely on a wire rack. *

✳

# Tattoo Cookies
### (chai-spiced + food-coloring-inked)
#### yields 24 cookies (depending on the size of the cutter)

I'm not a tattoo person and I don't come from tattoo people. Truth is, I love these unique expressions of individuality, and I'm in awe of the painstaking artwork devoted to the best designs, but I'll never surrender to the needle. What officially turned me off body ink for life is the recurring nightmare of a sinking heart on what was once a young girl's upper arm—but now hovers just above her elbow. Tattoos just never end up where they started. When I feel the urge to tattoo, I make these cookies instead.

3 ¾ cups all-purpose flour, sifted, plus more for dusting

1 teaspoon ground cinnamon

½ teaspoon ground ginger

½ teaspoon ground cardamom

¼ teaspoon freshly grated nutmeg

¼ teaspoon ground cloves

½ teaspoon freshly ground black pepper

½ teaspoon salt

1 teaspoon baking soda

1 cup (2 sticks) butter, at room temperature

1 cup packed light brown or dark brown sugar

½ cup honey

1 large egg, at room temperature

2 teaspoons vanilla paste

Food coloring, for painting the tattoos

*A little food coloring goes a long way. Have fun and always make sure to do one classic "Mom" heart tattoo . . . always.*

❶ In a medium mixing bowl, whisk together the flour, cinnamon, ginger, cardamom, nutmeg, cloves, pepper, salt, and baking soda. Set aside.

❷ In the bowl of a standing mixer fitted with the paddle attachment, beat the butter for 2 minutes, until smooth. Add the brown sugar and beat for 1 minute more, or until well combined. Add the honey and beat for another 3 minutes, or until light and fluffy. Add the egg and vanilla paste and beat until well incorporated. Reduce the speed to low and gradually beat in the flour mixture until fully blended. Remove the dough from the mixer, divide into two portions, and shape each into discs. Wrap the dough discs in plastic wrap and refrigerate for 4 hours, or until completely cold.

❸ Preheat the oven to 350° F. Line a baking sheet with parchment paper and set aside.

❹ Remove one dough disc from the refrigerator and roll out on a lightly floured surface to ¼ inch thick. You can also place the dough between two pieces of plastic wrap or waxed paper and roll out. Using hand and feet cookie cutters (or stencils you've made yourself and a paring knife), cut out the cookies. Place the cookies on the baking sheets about 1 inch apart. Gather up all the scraps and refrigerate them until you are ready to roll out and cut another baking sheet's worth of cookies.

❺ Bake for 10 to 12 minutes, until the cookies begin to turn golden brown around the edges. Continue baking cookies until all the dough has been used. Let the cookies cool completely before decorating.

❻ **To decorate:** Decide what tattoos you would like to paint on your cookies and place a couple drops of your chosen food colorings on a large plate (I like to use well-cleaned Styrofoam meat trays, the ones under the meat). Have a folded paper towel and glass of water available for cleaning the brush between colors. Using a very clean fine artist's brush, draw the outside of the tattoo first (I use blue food coloring for this). Once dry (don't worry, it will dry quickly), color the inside with your choice of food coloring. ✳

✳

# Root Beer Float Poppers

### (a classic summer treat you chew instead of sip)

yields 42 cookies

If you put ice in your root beer, there's a good chance we'll never be friends.

If you use vanilla ice cream in your root beer float, there's a good chance we could be friends.

If you use chocolate ice cream in your root beer float, there's a good chance we are friends.

If you use homemade chocolate ice cream in your IBC root beer float, there's a good chance we've slept together.

¾ cup (1 ½ sticks) butter, at room temperature

½ cup granulated sugar

1 large egg yolk

1 teaspoon root beer extract (I use McCormick)

1 ½ cups all-purpose flour

¼ cup dark unsweetened cocoa powder

¼ cup confectioners' sugar

½ cup crushed root beer barrel candies
(use a hammer to break up the candies, then finish in
a food processor to achieve an even consistency)

❶ In the bowl of a standing mixer fitted with the paddle attachment, cream together the butter and granulated sugar for 1 to 2 minutes, until light and fluffy. Add the egg yolk and root beer extract and beat until just combined.

❷ With the mixer on low speed, gradually add the flour and cocoa powder and mix until well incorporated. Refrigerate the dough for 30 minutes.

❸ Preheat the oven to 375° F. Line a baking sheet with parchment paper and set aside.

❹ Use a 1-tablespoon measure to scoop out the dough, then use your hands to shape the dough into balls. Place the balls on the prepared baking sheet 1 inch apart and bake for 6 to 10 minutes, or just until set. Meanwhile, combine the confectioners' sugar and crushed candies. When the poppers have cooled, roll them in the candy mixture. ✳

6

# canine goods

Gigi's PB & J Biscuits | Baked Chicken Liver Slivers

Maggie Jo's Red Velvet Dog Biscuits | Pumpkin Spice Canine Coins

Miles's Southern Squash Casserole Treats

*Unlike most store-bought dog biscuits, my dog biscuits are baked with such fresh ingredients that I like to refrigerate them to keep them fresh longer. Place baked and cooled treats in a zip-top bag and refrigerate for up to two weeks. The treats can be frozen in a zip-top bag for up to three months.*

★

*Nothing makes a dog owner happier than to be given a gift for their animal. For something simple, wrap the zip-top bag of treats in newspaper and tie with a ribbon the color of the dog's fur or eyes. For a more elaborate gift, use a chopstick or skewer to punch a hole in the treats before you bake them, and then use yarn or ribbon to string the treats together in a kind of canine candy necklace.*

Opposite: Maggie Jo's Red Velvet Dog Biscuits, page 190, and Baked Chicken Liver Slivers, page 192

＊

# Gigi's PB & J Biscuits

### (peanut butter, bacon, + beef jerky)

yields around 50 for a medium-sized dog, using a standard cookie cutter

Gigi Vero—my stripper name.

You know this party trick: Combine the name of your first pet and the name of the street where you first lived.

Gigi Marie Patrick was the name of my first pet. She was the sweetest charcoal gray poodle who was afraid of her own shadow and who, by the grace of God, went blind early so she wouldn't have to be afraid any longer.

Vero Drive was the street where I grew up—a short street lined with modest homes where Gigi and I ruled with kitchen towel capes tied tightly around our dirty necks.

I often bring up this silly parlor game around a dinner table filled with new and old friends. Undoubtedly, everyone laughs when they say the stripper name aloud, but it's the silence after that I find so moving. There is, always, a moment of silence. Always. A thoughtful remembrance for those animals in our lives that gave us endless amounts of unconditional love at our brightest and darkest times.

This short chapter of dog treats and stories is my way of saying "thank you" to all the unconditional love given to us by our animals. I've found when I watch someone sampling my baking, I get the same thrill out of seeing eyes roll back and hearing a moan as I do when I see a tail wag uncontrollably.

P.S. I wonder if my two sisters know that we all share the same stripper name?

2 ¼ cups whole wheat flour, plus more for dusting

1 tablespoon baking powder

¾ cup milk

1 large egg

1 cup natural peanut butter

2 slices bacon, cooked until crisp, chopped (rendered fat reserved and cooled)

¼ cup chopped mild beef jerky

❶ Preheat the oven to 325° F.

❷ Line a baking sheet with parchment paper and set aside.

❸ In the bowl of a standing mixer fitted with the paddle attachment, mix together the flour and baking powder. Add the remaining ingredients and mix until fully incorporated.

❹ Lightly flour a work surface and roll the dough out to ¼-inch thick. Use cookie cutters that are appropriate for the size of your dog, and cut the dough into shapes. Place the cut shapes on the prepared baking sheet and bake for 20 minutes. Turn the biscuits over and bake for an additional 15 minutes. Let cool completely. Store in a zip-top bag in the refrigerator for up to 1 month or in the freezer for up to 3 months. ＊

*Canine Goods*

*

# Baked Chicken Liver Slivers

### (canine fig newtons but with liver)

#### yields about 144

8 ounces chicken livers

½ cup chicken stock

2 large eggs

2 cups whole wheat flour

**1** Preheat the oven to 350° F. Spray a 9-by-12-inch baking pan with nonstick cooking spray and set aside.

**2** In the bowl of a food processor fitted with the blade attachment, combine the livers, stock, and eggs and process until smooth. Add the flour and pulse until combined. Pour the mixture into the prepared baking pan and smooth the top. Bake for 30 minutes, until the liver mixture is firm to the touch and dry on top.

**3** When the mixture has fully cooled, turn out onto a cutting board and use a long knife or pizza cutter to cut the treats into thirty-six (¼-inch-wide) long, thin strips. Then cut each strip into four equal pieces. Store in a zip-top bag in the refrigerator for up to 1 month or in the freezer for up to 3 months. Dogs love them at room temperature, cold, or frozen. *

For anyone who has ever accidentally stepped on a paw, these will be your redemption.

❊

# Maggie Jo's Red Velvet Dog Biscuits
## (beets, ham base, + whole wheat treats)

### yields around 50 for a medium-sized dog, using a standard cookie cutter

Maggie Jo is a Vizsla—a short-tempered, redheaded Hungarian bitch who has cost us a fortune. She has her own opinions, her own blog, and her own set of Tiffany pearls. After three short months of general gun-dog training, Maggie pointed and retrieved eight quail. Aside from love, the eight quail were the first things she has brought to the table. I'm told by her trainer and my husband that her quick progress is astounding. I would be more astounded if she could have cleaned and cooked the quail, too.

Maggie Jo is as smart as she is greedy. She attempts to take ownership (and often does!) of anything that enters our house. A book. A dress. A person. A cake. On my husband's birthday, just four months after Maggie Jo's first birthday, I was baking his traditional birthday cake—The.Best.Ever.Red.Velvet.Cake. (page 58). It became clear from her canine histrionics that Maggie Jo wanted the cake. Her pacing, steps away from the kitchen, didn't stop until the cake was crumb-coated and put in the refrigerator. They began again as the candles were lit and the traditional "Happy Birthday" song was sung. Of all her heady behavior, this was the weirdest. It was decided (by my husband) that Maggie Jo needed a red velvet treat of her own. So I indulged her and baked her these treats for her first Christmas. Then I baked them for her for first Valentine's Day, then her first Easter and then her second birthday. Basically, I've been baking them for her for most every holiday for the past year.

1 (15-ounce) can whole beets, drained;
or 6 roasted beets, peeled and quartered

½ teaspoon ham, chicken, or beef base
(highly concentrated stock; Maggie prefers ham)

1 large egg

2 ¼ to 2 ½ cups whole wheat flour, plus more for dusting

¾ cup dry milk powder

1 tablespoon baking powder

❶ Preheat the oven to 325° F.

❷ Line a baking sheet with parchment paper and set aside.

❸ In a blender, combine the beets, ham base, and egg and pulse until smooth.

❹ In a large mixing bowl, whisk together 2 ¼ cups flour, the dry milk powder, and baking powder. Stir the beet mixture into the flour mixture, using your hands to mix well. The dough should be very stiff. Add an additional ¼ cup flour if necessary.

❺ Lightly flour a work surface and roll out the dough to ¼ inch thick. Cut into desired sizes and shapes depending on the size of your dog. (Maggie likes a monogrammed biscuit, so I use an alphabet cookie cutter to cut an "M" in the middle of each biscuit.)

❻ Place the cut biscuits on the prepared baking sheet and bake for about 20 minutes. Turn the biscuits over and bake for an additional 15 minutes. Let the biscuits cool completely (about 30 minutes). Store in a zip-top bag in the refrigerator for up to 1 month or in the freezer for up to 3 months. ❊

❄

# Pumpkin Spice Canine Coins

## (a holiday pie for dogs)

### yields approximately 50

Use up any leftover mashed pumpkin from your holiday pie making to treat the four-legged members of your family.

2 ½ cups whole wheat flour, plus more for dusting

½ teaspoon ground cinnamon

2 large eggs

1 cup mashed fresh pumpkin (or use canned pure pumpkin puree; make sure to never use pumpkin pie mix, as the sugar and some of the spices are not good for dogs)

3 tablespoons natural peanut butter

❶ Preheat the oven to 350° F. Line a baking sheet with parchment paper and set aside.

❷ In the bowl of a standing mixer fitted with the paddle attachment, mix together the flour and cinnamon. Add the eggs, pumpkin, and peanut butter and beat until fully incorporated. Turn the dough out onto a lightly floured surface and roll out to ½ inch thick. Cut out coins using a 1- to 2-inch cookie cutter. (I use a small cutter because Maggie needs to watch her weight, but it all depends on the size of your dog.)

❸ Place on the prepared baking sheet and bake for 25 minutes, or until golden brown. Let cool completely. Store in a zip-top bag in the refrigerator for up to 1 month or in the freezer for up to 3 months. ❄

✳

# Miles's Southern Squash Casserole Treats

### (summer squash, butter crackers, + cheese)

#### yields about 100

Miles Patrick Summers: our first bird dog that we got as a married couple.

Miles was a holier-than-thou English Pointer, a particular eater who refused to sleep on anything that wasn't at least 400-thread count and could never be bothered to raise his voice to another canine unless it had blue eyes.

When Miles was three years old, our lives took us away from the grandeur and cold temperatures of the Rocky Mountains to a sleepy coastal town in North Carolina where we made an important discovery. Miles Patrick Summers was a Southern gentleman. He came alive in the sultry heat of the South, fearing no beast—snake, otter, or otherwise. In between long naps and sips of filtered water, his days were spent running circles around our small town as a self-appointed, four-legged mayor.

And, although his food hadn't changed, his zeal for it had. In Colorado, Miles would have to be enticed to eat. Nineteen hundred miles to the east, he was voracious. It's in his voracity to eat that we found he liked a favorite dish of the South—the traditional squash casserole. This discovery was made when a particular dish was covered and left on a table outside one of the town's eight churches—intended, of course, for a women's prayer circle meeting later that night. We were told it was found clean and empty on the ground when Miles was finished with it.

We prayed for the ladies' prayer circle members that night that they might find it in their hearts to forgive Miles. Judging by the cool reception he received for months after the casserole incident, they had not.

These biscuits are a tribute to Miles. He was an aristocrat, a true Southerner, and the love of our lives for six short years. He passed away with dignity, as only a gentleman would: riding in the back seat of a speeding Lincoln Town Car, on the way to an emergency veterinarian wrapped in an Hermès blanket with a monogram stitched in the corner. The monogram read M.P.S.

P.S. The ladies from the prayer circle group called after Miles's death to say they were praying for us to find peace through such a hard time. It was then that we realized the power of prayer. For a minute, we had a rest from our grief: We smiled when we thought how Miles would have much preferred a Southern squash casserole over their prayers.

*continued on page 196*

✳

## Miles's Southern Squash Casserole Treats, continued

1 cup cooked and mashed yellow summer squash

1 large egg

¼ cup vegetable stock or hot water

1 sleeve Ritz crackers, finely crushed

2 cups all-purpose flour, plus more for dusting

½ cup shredded cheddar cheese

❶ In a large mixing bowl, stir together the squash, egg, and stock. Add the crushed crackers and flour and stir unti well combined. Sprinkle with the cheese and work the cheese into the dough using your hands. Turn out onto a lightly floured work surface and roll into a 1-inch-diameter log. Wrap with plastic wrap and refrigerate for 30 minutes.

❷ Preheat the oven to 350° F.

❸ Line a baking sheet with parchment paper and set aside.

❹ Remove the dough from the refrigerator and slice into ¼-inch rounds. Place them on the baking sheet and bake for 15 minutes, or until hard. Let cool completely. Store in a zip-top bag in the refrigerator for up to 1 month or in the freezer for up to 3 months. ✳

Ellie Mae
can't eat just one.

# secret weapons

Every good baker has her own arsenal of sure-fire flavors and go-to methods for making dishes that will stand out on any table. If you ask what's the secret, the answer is typically modest: "Oh, it's nothing, really." Well, I'm here to tell you there is something, really, that makes a recipe outshine others. These are my own secret weapons of baking. These powerful little helpers pack a punch and lend a hand to almost any dish.

## extracts

Chemistry for Engineers.
The first college class I ever failed.
Partying for Engineers.
The first college class I ever got an A+ in.

If my college chemistry professor (for the life of me I can't remember his name) was now allowed a home visit, he'd open the doors to my cavernous kitchen pantry and see shelves lined with bottles and jars of various sizes all filled with colorful concoctions in contrasting stages of murkiness.

These are my own extracts and extract-blends steeping in the dark. Sugars infused with everything from vanilla to tea olive flowers. Detailed sketches, written notes, and dates meticulously noted in a lab book hang just inside the door.

It's no Chemistry for Engineers lab, but it's my own Chemistry for Cooks lab. I hate to admit it, but the professor I called a jerk under my breath as an eighteen-year-old was also the person who pushed me to succeed.

I had to retake Chemistry for Engineers. I earned a C. Partying for Engineers? Still an A+.

I challenge you to make a cake using regular sugar and store-bought extracts, and then make another using an infused sugar and a homemade extract. You'll find the infused sugars add layers of flavor to your cake. Not simply a sweet flavor, infused sugars give a hint of something extra that weaves through the batters and doughs you make. And, homemade extracts are smoother in flavor than a store-bought extract of the same name. They are subtle and a little sleepy—they don't overpower, they enhance flavor. In baking as in life, little things become the important details.

## Vanilla Extract
yields ½ cup

Cheese. Bourbon. Leather. Vanilla. Friends. All are time-tested, worth the wait, and get better with age.

**3 fresh (preferably organic) vanilla beans**

**½ cup vodka, rum, or bourbon**

Have a sterilized jar (run through a hot dishwasher cycle) with a tight-fitting lid ready.

With a sharp paring knife, starting ½ inch from the end of each vanilla bean, make a slit down one side without cutting all the way through the other side of the bean. Put the beans in the jar and pour the vodka over them. Screw the lid on tight and give it a good shake. Set aside in a dark place for 1 month, giving it a shake every few days. Strain into a clean sterilized jar and put the lid on tightly. Store the vanilla extract in a cool, dark place for up to 2 years. There is no need to refrigerate.

*Don't throw out your vanilla beans. Allow them to dry at room temperature then use them to make vanilla sugar (page 202).*

## Almond Extract

yields 1 cup

1 heaping cup roughly chopped raw almonds

1 cup vodka

Have a sterilized jar (run through a hot dishwasher cycle) with a tight-fitting lid ready.

Put the nuts in the jar and pour the vodka over them. Screw the lid on tight and give it a good shake. Set aside in a dark place for 1 month, giving it a shake every few days. Strain into a clean sterilized jar and put the lid on tightly. Store the almond extract in a cool, dark place for up to 1 year. There is no need to refrigerate.

## Star Anise Extract

yields ½ cup

½ cup star anise

½ cup vodka

Have a sterilized ½ pint jar (run through a hot dishwasher cycle) with a tight-fitting lid ready.

Put the star anise in the jar and pour the vodka over it. Screw the lid on tight and give it a good shake. Set aside in a dark place for 3 to 4 months, giving it a good shake once a week. Strain into a clean sterilized jar and put the lid on tightly. Store the star anise extract in a cool, dark place for up to 1 year. There is no need to refrigerate.

## Hot Pepper Extract

yields 1 cup

1 serrano chile, stem removed, cut in half lengthwise

2 jalapeño chiles, stems removed, cut lengthwise into strips

1 cup vodka

Have a sterilized jar (run through a hot dishwasher cycle) with a tight-fitting lid ready.

Put the chiles in the jar and pour the vodka over them. Screw the lid on tight and give it a good shake. Set aside in a dark place for 1 month, giving it a shake every few days. Strain into a clean sterilized jar and put the lid on tightly. Store the hot pepper extract in a cool, dark place for up to 1 year. There is no need to refrigerate.

## Lavender Extract

yields ½ cup

3 tablespoons dried pesticide-free lavender buds

½ cup vodka

Have a sterilized jar (run through a hot dishwasher cycle) with a tight-fitting lid ready.

Put the lavender buds in the jar and pour the vodka over them. Screw the lid on tight and give it a good shake. Set aside in a dark place for 2 weeks, giving it a shake every few days. Strain into a clean sterilized jar and put the lid on tightly. Store the lavender extract in a cool, dark place for up to 2 years. There is no need to refrigerate.

*Be aware that this stuff is pungent—a little goes a long way in a recipe.*

## Lemon Extract

yields 1 cup

2 large organic lemons, scrubbed clean and dried

1 cup naturally flavored lemon vodka (I use Hangar One Citron Buddha's Hand), or plain vodka

Have a sterilized jar (run through a hot dishwasher cycle) with a tight-fitting lid ready.

Using a vegetable peeler, peel the lemons so you get only the yellow rind, avoiding the white part of the peel, which will make the extract bitter. Cut the rind into thin strips, put them in the jar, and pour the vodka over them. Screw the lid on tight and give it a good shake. Set aside in a dark place for 1 month, giving it a shake every few days. Strain into a clean sterilized jar and put the lid on tightly. Store

the lemon extract in a cool, dark place for up to 1 year. There is no need to refrigerate.

## Orange Extract

yields 1 cup

2 large organic navel oranges, scrubbed clean and dried

1 cup naturally flavored orange vodka (I use Hangar One Mandarin Blossom), or plain vodka

Have a sterilized jar (run through a hot dishwasher cycle) with a tight-fitting lid ready.

Using a vegetable peeler, peel the oranges so you get only the orange rind, avoiding the white part of the peel, which will make the extract bitter. Cut the rind into thin strips, put them in the jar, and pour the vodka over them. Screw the lid on tight and give it a good shake. Set aside in a dark place for 1 month, giving it a shake every few days. Strain into a clean sterilized jar and put the lid on tightly. Store the orange extract in a cool, dark place for up to 1 year. There is no need to refrigerate.

## S&V House Blend Almond Extract

yields 1 ounce

A smoother, gentler almond extract.

4 ½ teaspoons vanilla extract

1 ½ teaspoons almond extract

Put the extracts in a small, lidded bottle and shake gently to combine. Label the bottle and store in a cool, dark place for up to 1 year. There is no need to refrigerate.

## S&V House Blend Citrus Extract

yields 1 ounce

**I like secrets. I can't keep one to save my life, but I still like them nonetheless. This recipe is my take on the secret Sicilian recipe for Fiori di Sicilia (flowers of Sicily) extract. The centuries-old original is a highly fragrant secret blend of vanilla, citrus, and flower essences**

that's been used to flavor all sorts of sweet foods. When I add a little of my version to a recipe, it's akin to adding a Sicilian to my dinner-party guest list. It makes everything much livelier.

3 teaspoons vanilla extract (page 198)

1 ½ teaspoons orange extract (page 199)

1 ½ teaspoons lemon extract (page 199)

Put the extracts in a small, lidded bottle and shake gently to combine. Label the bottle and store in a cool, dark place for up to 1 year. There is no need to refrigerate. ✳

## Bottles

You've probably noticed I don't like anything too ordinary in my life or in my kitchen. The bottles I use when making my homemade extracts are no exception. Nothing makes me happier than to flip on the light in my cool, dark pantry and see all my beautiful extracts steeping inside bottles of varying shapes and sizes. Most are repurposed after being emptied of whatever originally came in them (like syrup, soda, or liquor) and sterilized in the dishwasher. It's best to use a bottle with a tight-fitting lid so you can give the contents a good shake as needed, but if you have an unlidded bottle you love, don't let that stop you from using it. One of my favorite bottles that I use again and again for making lavender extract has no lid. As a stopper tied to the top, I use a buckeye nut that I picked up on the grounds of the Luxembourg Gardens in Paris. Lavender always reminds me of my travels through France, and this little gem makes the bottle—and its contents—even more special.

## Gift Ideas

Homemade extracts are my favorite hostess gifts. I like to go to the liquor store and purchase miniature bottles of liquor that have interesting shapes to package the extracts in. Just empty the contents (preferably into a cocktail) and run the bottle through a hot cycle in the dishwasher before filling with your homemade extract. One of my favorite bottles is the one St. Germain (an elderflower liqueur) is sold in. Its shape reminds me of a man's body— wide shoulders and a small thin frame . . .

but I digress. Whatever you do, make sure you include one of your favorite recipes using the extract—that's what makes a gift special. Over the years, I've found that the man-shaped bottle alone won't do it.

## Extracts in Cleaning

Having worked for years cooking aboard large sailing yachts, I've cleaned more than my share of surfaces in the cabins below deck. About a year into that career, I developed my own recipe for the perfect wood and surface cleaner, and I still use it today in my own home. In a large spray bottle, shake together 4 cups water, ½ cup white vinegar, and 1 tablespoon homemade extract. The extract masks the scent of the vinegar and is an aromatherapeutic. Depending where I may be cleaning, I change the extract to inform the mood of the room. In a bedroom, I use lavender extract for a peaceful, calming scent. In a living room or kitchen I use orange or lemon extract for a more awakening scent.

## Extracts in Cocktails

Remember when people went to bartender schools? The notion of getting a "bartender's certificate" always made me giggle. But, knowing what flavors work together on a plate is the same skill as knowing what flavors work together in a glass, right? Using homemade extracts is a great way to create specialty drinks.

## Sweet Orange Home Slice

makes 1 drink

½ teaspoon orange extract (page 199)

2 ounces vodka

4 ounces club soda

1 orange slice candy

In a shaker filled with ice, combine all the ingredients except the candy. Shake lightly. Fill a rocks glass with fresh ice and top with an orange slice candy. Strain the contents of the shaker over the candy and into the glass.

## French Kiss

makes 1 drink

¼ teaspoon lavender extract (page 199)

2 ounces vodka

1 teaspoon honey

Juice of ½ lime

Seltzer

1 sprig fresh lavender

In a highball glass filled with ice, combine the lavender extract, honey, and lime juice. Fill the glass with seltzer and stir gently. Garnish with the lavender sprig. ✳

## Lemon Head

makes 1 drink

½ teaspoon lemon extract (page 199)

2 ounces vodka

2 ounces sweet and sour mix

Seltzer

Lemonhead candies

In a tall glass filled with ice, combine the lemon extract, vodka, and sweet and sour mix. Fill the glass with seltzer and stir gently. Garnish with candies. ✳

## Vanilla Cake

makes 1 drink

⅛ teaspoon vanilla extract (page 198)
2 ounces vodka
Ginger ale
Colored sugar sprinkles

In a rocks glass filled with ice, combine the vanilla extract and vodka. Fill the glass with ginger ale and stir gently. Garnish with sugar sprinkles. ✳

# infused sugars

## Vanilla Sugar

yields 3 cups

If you make only one infused sugar, please let it be this one.

You'll find my vanilla sugar used in recipes throughout this book. I'm obsessed with how it adds a layer of subtle flavor to a recipe. I'm a believer that if you try vanilla sugar in one recipe, you'll keep reaching for it again and again. Vanilla sugar is great for sweetening beverages. Add a little to your hot or iced tea. Or, the next time you make your favorite lemonade recipe (mine also involves caramelizing the lemons with vanilla sugar before I squeeze them), substitute vanilla sugar for the regular sugar. You can thank me later.

1 fresh (preferably organic) vanilla bean

3 cups sugar

Have a sterilized 1-quart jar (run through a hot dishwasher) with a tight-fitting lid ready.

Using a sharp paring knife, cut a slit down one side of the vanilla bean, scrape out the seeds, and place the seeds and bean in the jar. Fill the jar with 2 cups of the sugar. Screw the lid on tightly and give it a good shake. Remove the lid and top off the jar with the remaining 1 cup sugar. Screw the lid on tightly then label and date the jar. Set aside in a cool, dry pantry for 2 weeks to achieve peak flavor before using (although I've been known to use it after just 2 days). Keep adding more sugar to the jar as you use it. One vanilla bean should last through 3 jars (9 cups) sugar and the sugar will keep indefinitely.

## Clove Sugar

yields 3 cups

Try this sugar in holiday recipes for pies (filling and dough), sweet potato pancakes, spice cakes, or wherever you want to add an extra pop of flavor. I use it as a one-to-one substitute for regular sugar in recipes.

2 tablespoons whole cloves

3 cups sugar

Have a sterilized 1-quart jar (run through a hot dishwasher cycle) with a tight-fitting lid ready.

In a medium bowl, toss together the cloves and sugar. Spoon the mixture into the prepared jar and seal tightly. Label and date the jar. Set aside in a cool, dry place for 2 weeks to 1 month. Pour the contents through a colander to remove the whole cloves. Return the clove sugar to the jar and seal tightly. Store in a cool, dark place for up to 6 months.

## Lavender Sugar

yields 3 cups

Every Bastille day I do three things:

1. I blast "Zou Bisou Bisou" (one of my Mother's favorite songs) as loud as I can.

2. I mix up three quarts of Lavender Sugar.

3. I thank heaven I'm an American citizen.

Cakes, cookies, waffles, or iced-tea—lavender sugar adds just a little "Zou Bisou Bisou" to most anything you can imagine. Best when used within one year of Bastille Day.

1 tablespoon dried (pesticide-free) lavender buds

3 cups sugar

Have a sterilized 1-quart jar (run through a hot dishwasher cycle) with a tight-fitting lid ready.

Using a mortar and pestle, crush the lavender buds together with 2 tablespoons of the sugar. Put the crushed mixture in a medium mixing bowl and stir in the remaining sugar. Spoon the mixture into the prepared jar and screw the lid on tightly. Label and date the jar. Set aside in a cool, dry place for 2 weeks before using. Store in a cool, dark place for up to 1 year.

## Star Anise Sugar

yields 3 cups

½ cup star anise

3 cups sugar

Have a sterilized 1-quart jar (run through a hot dishwasher cycle) with a tight-fitting lid ready.

In a medium mixing bowl, toss together the star anise and sugar. Spoon the mixture into the prepared jar and seal tightly. Label and date the jar. Set aside in a cool, dry place for 1 month. Sift through a colander to remove the star anise. Return the sugar to the jar and seal tightly. Store in a cool, dark place for up to 6 months.

## Red Pepper Flake Sugar

yields 3 cups

This is a Sweet and Vicious building block.

3 teaspoons red pepper flakes

3 cups sugar

Have a sterilized 1-quart jar (run through a hot dishwasher cycle) with a tight-fitting lid ready.

Use a mortar and pestle or food processor to pulverize 2 teaspoons of the red pepper flakes with 2 tablespoons of the sugar. Put the pulverized mixture in a medium mixing bowl and stir in the remaining red pepper flakes and sugar. Spoon the mixture into the prepared jar and screw the lid on tightly. Label and date the jar. Set aside in a cool, dry place for 2 weeks to 1 month before using. For a milder flavor, you can sift through a fine-mesh colander before using. (I like all things hotter, so I leave it as it is.) Store in a cool, dark place for up to 6 months.

## Tea Olive Blossom Sugar

yields ½ cup

Closing the cultural gap sometimes just takes a flower and an apology.

If you live in a warm climate, there's a good possibility you will have smelled the sweet scent of the tea olive bush (*Osmanthus fragrans*) when it blooms. The scent is a cross between rose and jasmine, with a kiss of gardenia. In the American South, it's customary to plant tea olive bushes near swinging screen doors and open windows so on breezy days in the late winter months their fragrance fills the home. I have six planted in my small yard.

Content to enjoy the tea olive's scent alone, I was curious when my friend Chia Chong (the photographer of this very book you're reading) said her mother cooks with the blossoms. "Cook with the blossoms? Are times so tough in Malaysia that your mother has to make dinner from ornamental bushes?" I asked.

Per usual, Chia held her tongue and allowed my small Western mind to digest the idea.

Two days later I was online watching enough Chinese chefs making desserts with tea olive blossom–infused sugar that I swore I could speak Mandarin.

Three days later I was making tea olive blossom–infused sugar myself.

Four days later I was formally apologizing to Chia and her mom.

½ cup fresh tea olive blossoms, stems removed (try not to handle the blossoms too much with your fingers, as they brown quickly)

½ cup sugar

Have a sterilized 1-pint jar (run through a hot dishwasher cycle) with a tight-fitting lid ready.

Submerge the blossoms in cold water and pat dry with a paper towel.

Layer the blossoms and sugar in equal measurements in the prepared jar. Screw the lid on tightly the label and date the jar. Set aside in a cool, dry place for 2 to 3 weeks, shaking the jar every day until the sugar becomes a syrup. Store in a cool, dark place for up to 3 months. There is no need to refrigerate.

*If you like immediate gratification, put the sugar, tea olive blossoms, and 1 tablespoon water in a small saucepan. Cook over very low heat, stirring constantly, until the sugar dissolves. Remove from the heat and let cool completely. Add additional water for your desired syrup consistency.*

*Try using tea olive syrup in any recipe instead of maple syrup. In addition to my baking recipes, I really love tea olive syrup in barbecue sauces, in salad dressings, and dripping off the end of a fork attached to a big piece of warm buttermilk pancake.*

## Showy Sugar Cubes

yields 40

These cheeky colored sugar cubes are quite proud. They prefer nothing less than to be crushed and sprinkled atop a cookie before baking, or used whole to decorate a frosted cake (with a broken Rubik's cube kind of randomness), or simply served alongside after-dinner espressos for a pop of sweet color. Make several batches in different colors.

1 cup sugar

¼ teaspoon liquid food coloring (see Note)

Preheat the oven to 250° F.

Line the bottom of an 8-by-4-inch loaf pan with parchment paper. (You can use a 9-by-5-inch loaf pan, but your sugar cubes will be a little thinner.) Set aside.

Put the sugar in a small mixing bowl and pour the food coloring and 2 ¾ teaspoons water (3 teaspoons water if you're making white sugar cubes) into the center of the sugar. Mix with a fork until the color is fully integrated and there are no lumps in the sugar (the mixture will have the consistency of wet sand). Pour the sugar mixture into the prepared pan and use the back of the fork to make it level. Compact the sugar by tamping down with whatever you have that's flat and heavy. I like to use a heavy pie server because it can get into the corners easily. Keep tamping until the sugar is very compact and you have removed a lot of air.

Using a sharp knife, slowly cut the sugar into squares by cutting into 4 long strips then 10 shorter strips. For an 8-by-4-inch loaf pan you should get 40 cubes that are ½ inch thick.

Bake for 1 hour. Remove from the oven and allow to cool on the countertop until the pan is cool enough to handle, 5 to 10 minutes. Invert the pan to remove the sugar cubes and break apart with your hands. Allow to cool completely. Store the cubes in an airtight container out of direct sunlight. Cubes will keep for up to 1 year.

*I use liquid food coloring here rather than paste because it mixes more easily into the water and sugar.*

# frostings

Jewelry is like frosting. It catches the eye and puts the finishing touch on an outfit. A good frosting dresses up an otherwise pedestrian cake. You might even say frostings are worth their weight in gold, or silver, or platinum . . . I'm not picky.

## INTERNATIONAL BUTTERCREAM GUIDE

### AMERICAN
The standard in commercial frostings because it's easy to make, great for piping, and can stand up in almost all environmental conditions. A mixture of two fats (butter and vegetable shortening) and confectioners' sugar. Super sweet.

### ITALIAN
Made with more egg whites than Swiss Meringue Buttercream, it is light and smooth in flavor. Italian Meringue is probably the most durable of all the

buttercream frostings. The only issue is it is not necessarily 100 percent food-safe since the egg whites never reach the temperature that kills bacteria (160° F).

## FRENCH

The use of egg yolk in the recipe makes for a denser finished product but still very silky, with an über-buttery taste.

## SWISS MERINGUE

Very similar to Italian Meringue Buttercream using egg whites heated in a hot sugar syrup, but way easier to make and 100 percent food-safe. I love Swiss Meringue!

# My American Buttercream Frosting

(all-butter buttercream)

yields about 5 cups

Typically an American buttercream frosting uses two types of fat—butter and vegetable shortening—so it can hold up better under adverse temperatures. Mine uses all butter for a bigger butter flavor . . . heat be damned.

2 cups (4 sticks) butter, at room temperature

6 to 8 cups confectioners' sugar, sifted

½ teaspoon salt

1 tablespoon vanilla paste

4 to 8 tablespoons evaporated milk

In the bowl of a standing mixer fitted with the paddle attachment, beat the butter on medium speed until creamy. Reduce the speed to low and gradually add 6 cups of the confectioners' sugar. Increase the speed to medium and add the salt, vanilla paste, and 4 tablespoons of the evaporated milk. Beat for 2 minutes. If the frosting is too thin at this point, add more of the confectioners' sugar, ½ cup at a time, and beat for 1 minute, until fully incorporated. If the frosting is too thick, add more of the evaporated milk, 1 tablespoon at a time, and beat for 30 seconds or until just combined. Refrigerate the frosting for 20 minutes before using. Frosting can be made ahead and stored in the refrigerator for up to 1 week.

This frosting is great with any of these recipes:

Good and Plenty Cupcakes (page 18)
Salty Pumpkin Spice Cake (page 21)
Girly-Girl Lavender Cake (page 29)
Fairground Attraction Cake (page 34)
Hog Heaven Chocolate Cake (page 44)
Lemonhead Cake (page 50)

# Swiss Meringue Buttercream Frosting

(easy, buttery, and stable)

yields about 5 cups

I'm not neutral about Swiss Meringue Buttercream. Aside from My American Buttercream, it's my go-to frosting. Unlike My American version that is all butter and can occasionally end up running down the side of a cake on a hot day, this frosting holds up well under most adverse environmental conditions. It's also, despite the precision implied by "Swiss," one of the easiest buttercreams to make. And, you don't need a Swiss Army knife to make it . . .

5 large egg whites

1 ½ cups sugar

1 ½ pounds (6 sticks) butter, cut into chunks, at room temperature

1 tablespoon vanilla extract (page 198)

Fill a medium saucepan with 2 inches water and place over medium-low heat. Set a medium ovenproof bowl over the simmering water, making sure the bottom of the bowl doesn't come into contact with the water. Put the egg whites and sugar in the bowl and whisk together until all the sugar crystals have dissolved. Pour the hot egg white mixture into the (room temperature) bowl of a standing mixer fitted with the whisk attachment. Whisk on high speed for 10 minutes, or until the meringue has doubled in volume, holds a stiff peak, and has cooled down. It's important that the meringue is not warm, or it will melt the butter. I usually stick my finger down into the meringue to feel the temp—and get a taste!

Remove the whisk attachment and replace it with the paddle attachment. Mix the butter into the cooled meringue, ½ cup at a time.

*It is important to beat just until the butter is incorporated into the meringue; I prefer to turn the mixer off and on to create a pulsing effect. Once all the butter has been incorporated, gradually increase the speed of the mixer to high, then continue to beat on high speed until the mixture is thick and fluffy and holds a stiff peak. (Don't be alarmed. The mixture will get soft and limp and then it will perk right up in a minute or two. I'm talking about the frosting—get your mind out of the gutter!) Scrape down the bowl as needed. Reduce the speed to low and add the vanilla, then beat for 1 more minute on high speed.*

Leftover frosting will keep in an airtight container in the refrigerator for up to 3 weeks and in the freezer for up to 3 months. Thaw completely and rewhip before using.

*Try flavoring your Swiss Meringue Buttercream Frosting with different extracts such as lemon or almond (pages 199 and 198; I use a one-to-one ratio in place of the vanilla). Or try a little alcohol such as a dark rum or ouzo. Or just drink the rum and ouzo and don't mess with perfection.*

This frosting is great with any of these recipes:

Lemonhead Cake (page 50)
Good and Plenty Cupcakes (page 18)
Girly-Girl Lavender Cake (page 29)
Fairground Attraction Cake (page 34)
Hog Heaven Chocolate Cake (page 44)

*Don't be alarmed if your Swiss Meringue Frosting curdles, nothing is lost. The curdling is happening because the butter you added, was cooler than the meringue. Just keep beating and it will all come together.*

# Cream Cheese Frosting

(the world's best. period.)

yields about 6 cups

Warning! The information you are about to receive is a Game Changer.

I try to buy organic as much as I can. And, in my own gardens, it's the only way I grow. And yet, with all that crunchy intention, this is the only recipe in my life that I insist on being completely organic. You have to trust me on this; the organic ingredients used in this cream cheese frosting result in a slightly different flavor—more earthy, more sour, more smooth. Using them will change your cake, your cinnamon rolls, and your life.

1 cup (2 sticks) organic butter, at room temperature

3 (8-ounce) packages organic cream cheese, at room temperature

1 teaspoon organic vanilla paste

4 cups organic confectioners' sugar, sifted (sifting is a must!)

In the bowl of a standing mixer fitted with the paddle attachment, cream together the butter and cream cheese. Add the vanilla paste and mix thoroughly. Add the confectioners' sugar 1 cup at a time, beating until each addition is incorporated before adding the next. Scrape down the bowl as needed. Use immediately. If the frosting becomes too soft, pop it in the refrigerator for 20 to 30 minutes, until it is a spreadable consistency. Frosting can be made ahead and stored in the refrigerator for up to 1 week.

This frosting is great with any of these recipes:

Best. Ever. Red. Velvet. Cake. (page 58)
Habañero Carrot Cake (page 32)
Solid Gold Beet Cupcakes (page 42)
Salvation Cinnamon Rolls (page 62)
Salty Pumpkin Spice Cake (page 21)
Spice Channel Cake (page 52)

# Marshmallow Frosting

(fluffy, sticky, sexy, and sweet)

yields about 4 cups

8 large egg whites, at room temperature

2 cups sugar

½ teaspoon cream of tartar

1 teaspoon vanilla extract (page 198)

Fill a medium saucepan with 2 inches water and place over medium-low heat. Set the bowl from a standing mixer over the simmering water, making sure the bottom of the bowl doesn't come into contact with the water. If you're not using a standing mixer, a heatproof stainless-steel bowl will work fine. Put the egg whites, sugar, and cream of tartar in the bowl and whisk constantly for 4 minutes, until the sugar dissolves and the mixture is warm.

Transfer the bowl to the standing mixer fitted with the whisk attachment (or use a hand mixer) and whisk for 5 to 7 minutes, gradually increasing the speed until stiff, glossy peaks form. Add the vanilla extract and mix until just combined. Frosting should be used immediately.

This frosting is great with any of these recipes:

Post-Coital Pie (page 130)
Best. Ever. Red. Velvet. Cake. (page 58)
Hog Heaven Chocolate Cake (page 44)

# Caramel Cream Cheese Frosting

(crazy creamy good)

yields about 5 cups

Frostings are the upscale accessories of the baking world. I believe that with the right frosting (like the right accessory for an outfit), a good cake can become great, and a great cake can become epic. Take the stack of Hermès bangles I've collected over the years—they can make a simple T-shirt and jeans look chic. I feel the same way about my Caramel Cream Cheese Frosting. When I put a dollop of that frosting on a humdrum December strawberry, I want to photograph it! I want to write a book about it! So I have.

1 cup (2 sticks) butter

2 cups dark brown sugar

½ cup milk

12 ounces cream cheese, at room temperature

4 cups confectioners' sugar, sifted

1 teaspoon vanilla paste

In a medium saucepan over low heat, melt the butter. Stir in the brown sugar and cook, stirring constantly, for 2 minutes. Increase the heat to medium and stir in the milk. Continue to cook, stirring occasionally, until the mixture comes to a boil and the sugar has completely dissolved. Remove from the heat and let cool to room temperature.

In the bowl of a standing mixer fitted with the paddle attachment, beat the cream cheese until smooth. Add the cooled caramel mixture and beat until combined. Add the confectioners' sugar 1 cup at a time, beating until each addition is incorporated before adding the next. Scrape down the sides of the bowl as needed. Add the vanilla paste and beat for 1 minute.

Leftovers can be refrigerated for up to 10 days or frozen for up to 3 months. When you are ready to use, bring to room temperature and beat until creamy. Add a little confectioners' sugar if needed to bring the frosting back to a creamy consistency.

*If you'd like to kick up the heat, add a pinch of cayenne pepper to the finished frosting.*

This frosting is great with any of these recipes:

Salvation Cinnamon Rolls (page 62)
Salty Pumpkin Spice Cake (page 21)
Habañero Carrot Cake (page 32)
Solid Gold Beet Cupcakes (page 42)
Spice Channel Cake (page 52)

# Caramel Frosting

(short-cut caramel)

yields about 3 cups

This recipe is my version of an "instant gratification" caramel frosting. I cheat a little and start with brown sugar. I love caramel frosting so much I had to figure out a way to make it fast so I could get to eating it faster. No, I do not make a traditional caramel base like my "Cheffy McPastry Chef" friend David Lebovitz would. But while David is waiting for his caramel to finish cooking, he could be enjoying a slice of my finished cake.

1 cup (2 sticks) butter

2 cups light brown sugar

½ cup milk

4 cups confectioners' sugar, sifted

1 teaspoon vanilla paste

In a medium saucepan over low heat, melt the butter. Stir in the brown sugar and cook, stirring constantly, for 2 minutes. Stir in the milk and continue stirring until the mixture comes to boil, then remove from the heat and let cool slightly. Transfer the mixture to the bowl of a standing mixer fitted with the whisk attachment and whisk in the confectioners' sugar 1 cup at a time, whisking until each addition is incorporated before adding the next. Scrape down the sides of the bowl as needed. Add the vanilla paste and beat for 1 minute.

Frost your cake while the frosting and the cake are both still warm.

This frosting is great with any of these recipes:

Salty Pumpkin Spice Cake (page 21)
Habañero Carrot Cake (page 32)
Hog Heaven Chocolate Cake (page 44)
Salvation Cinnamon Rolls (page 62)
Solid Gold Beet Cupcakes (page 42)

# Rich Chocolate Buttercream Frosting

(dark and decadent)

yields about 3 ½ cups

As a young mother, I used to save any leftover chocolate buttercream frosting and make my son quick no-bake cookies for a special treat. Like most simple things, I'd make a full-blown theatrical production out of spreading a thin layer of the frosting between two graham crackers. He believed it was chocolate magic and would tell me I was the best mom in the world.

Did it bother me that these rare accolades were likely the result of a sugar high? Of course not! A mom takes what she can get.

1 cup (2 sticks) butter, at room temperature

½ cup good-quality unsweetened cocoa powder, sifted (better chocolate = better frosting)

3 ½ to 4 cups confectioners' sugar, sifted

½ teaspoon salt

8 to 10 tablespoons heavy cream

1 teaspoon vanilla paste

In the bowl of a standing mixer fitted with the paddle attachment, beat the butter until light and creamy. Turn off the mixer and stir in the cocoa powder and 3 ½ cups of the confectioners' sugar. Resume mixing on low speed for 3 minutes, until all the cocoa and confectioners' sugar have been incorporated into the butter. Add the salt, 8 tablespoons of the cream, and the vanilla paste. Beat on medium speed for 2 minutes, until creamy. If the frosting is too thick, add a bit more cream, 1 tablespoon at a time, and beat for 30 seconds or until just combined. If the frosting is too thin, add a bit more confectioners' sugar, ½ cup at a time, and beat for 1 minute until fully incorporated. Frosting can be made ahead and stored in the refrigerator for up to 1 week.

This frosting is great with any of these recipes:

Hog Heaven Chocolate Cake (page 44)
Solid Gold Beet Cupcakes (page 42)
Fairground Attraction Cake (page 34)
Girly- Girl Lavender Cake (page 29)
Lemonhead Cake (page 50)
Jalapeño "Sort of" Shortbread Cookies (page 174)

# Guava Buttercream Frosting

(tropical sweet buttercream)

yields about 4 cups

I was hooked on guava from the first time I tasted it while traveling in Mexico. The thick-skinned fruit with a kind of strawberry flavor was served sliced with a heavy pinch of salt and pepper. When I returned home to the United States, I started experimenting with guava paste (guava fruit cooked with sugar) in my recipes—minus the black pepper—and I found it tasted great with nearly every cake.

2 cups (4 sticks) butter, at room temperature

¾ cup guava paste, at room temperature

2 cups confectioners' sugar, sifted

½ teaspoon salt

½ teaspoon vanilla paste

In the bowl of a standing mixer fitted with the paddle attachment, beat the butter and guava paste on medium speed for 1 minute, or until the guava paste is fully incorporated into the butter and the mixture becomes creamy. Reduce the speed to low and gradually add 2 cups of the confectioners' sugar. Scrape down the bowl as needed. Increase the speed to medium and add the salt and vanilla paste. Beat for 2 minutes. Refrigerate the frosting for 10 minutes before using. Frosting can be made ahead and stored in the refrigerator for up to 1 week.

*Guava is high in natural pectin, so if you are a first time jelly or jam maker it's a great fruit to start with. It's very forgiving.*

This frosting is great with any of these recipes:

Coconut Fluff Cake (page 40)
Salvation Cinnamon Rolls (page 62)
Solid Gold Beet Cupcakes (page 42)
Fairground Attraction Cake (page 34)

# Kiss Me Frosting

(cinnamon buttercream)

yields about 3 ½ cups

I get weak in the knees when I think about how powerful this frosting is. I have found nothing—nothing—that it doesn't taste good on. Biscuits, baby cakes, bacon, and my husband's sweet lips.

1 cup (2 sticks ) butter, at room temperature

4 ½ cups confectioners' sugar, sifted

¼ teaspoon salt

1 teaspoon vanilla paste

2 tablespoons evaporated milk

⅛ teaspoon red food coloring

1 (6-ounce) box Red Hots cinnamon candies, pulsed in a food processor to crush

In the bowl of a standing mixer fitted with the paddle attachment, beat the butter on medium speed until fluffy. Reduce the speed to low and gradually add the confectioners' sugar. Increase the speed to medium and add the salt, vanilla paste, and evaporated milk. Beat for 2 minutes. If the frosting is too thin at this point you can add more of the confectioners' sugar and mix for 30 seconds, or just until combined. If the frosting is too thick, add a bit more evaporated milk, 1 tablespoon at a time, and mix for 30 seconds, or just until combined. Add the food coloring and mix until fully incorporated. Remove the bowl and use a spatula to fold in the crushed cinnamon candies. Refrigerate the frosting for 10 minutes before using. Frosting can be made ahead and stored in the refrigerator for up to one week.

This frosting is great with any of these recipes:

Hot & Heavy Baby Cakes (page 36)
Best. Red. Velvet. Cake. Ever. (page 58)
Fairground Attraction Cake (page 34)
Salvation Cinnamon Rolls (page 62)

# Mascarpone Frosting

(Italian and spiced)

yields about 4 cups

Mascarpone is the well-educated Italian cousin of our American cream cheese. Although similar in texture, its triple-creamed process gives mascarpone a richer flavor than cream cheese.

16 ounces mascarpone cheese, at room temperature

1 cup (2 sticks) butter, at room temperature

½ teaspoon ground cinnamon

¼ teaspoon ground cardamom

2 to 3 cups confectioners' sugar, sifted

1 teaspoon vanilla paste

Using a hand mixer in a large mixing bowl, beat the mascarpone and butter until just smooth. Add the cinnamon and cardamom and mix until just incorporated. Mix in 2 cups of the confectioners' sugar and continue beating until smooth. Add the vanilla paste and beat until just combined. If the frosting is too thin, add the additional 1 cup confectioners' sugar and mix for 30 seconds until fully incorporated. Frosting can be made ahead and stored in the refrigerator for up to one week.

This frosting is great with any of these recipes:

Spice Channel Cake (page 52)
Habañero Carrot Cake (page 32)
Solid Gold Beet Cupcakes (page 42)
Salvation Cinnamon Rolls (page 62)

# S&V Royal Icing

yields about 3 ½ cups

3 large egg whites

4 cups confectioners' sugar, sifted

1 teaspoon S&V House Blend Citrus Extract (page 199)

6 different food colorings
(use whatever colors you love)

Have seven small bowls and seven toothpicks ready.

In the bowl of a standing mixer fitted with the paddle attachment, beat the egg whites for 1 to 2 minutes, until soft peaks form. Gradually add the confectioners' sugar, 1 cup at a time, and continue to beat. Add the citrus extract and beat for 8 minutes, or until stiff peaks form.

Divide the icing among the seven bowls and color six of the icings with whatever different colors you love. Leave one bowl for white icing. (If you couldn't tell, I love bright colors! I used 4 to 6 drops of each food coloring and a small spoon to stir.)

To make a thinner, flood icing (so named because it floods the area between the thicker frosting outline) for the colors, stir in ½ teaspoon water at a time until the icing reaches a thin consistency. Cover the icings with plastic wrap until you are ready to use.

# ingredients arsenal

Use only the best ingredients you can find or afford. Why? Because fresh, organic, farm-raised, or homegrown foods have a richer, deeper flavor.

## Butter

Great butter is made from sweet cream that comes from pasture-grazed cattle. Simply put, it's the varied diet that cows eat that gives butter a richer flavor and aroma–the slight tang with a nuttiness is what I love. It's also the level of craftsmanship that goes into the butter-making that makes a difference in quality: The speed at which the cream is cooled after pasteurization affects the texture and smoothness of the butter. I've made my own butter in the past and decided I'd rather spend my time baking. Look for grade AA butter, organic if possible from your local farmers' market.

*All the recipes in Sweet & Vicious use unsalted butter. I never use a salted butter. Never. I like to be in control of the amount of salt going into a recipe.*

## Clarified Butter

Clarifying butter is the process of removing the water and milk solids from the butterfat. This yields a clear golden fat that stands up to higher temperatures. I always like to have a jar of clarified butter in the refrigerator for frying eggs in the morning. The process is easy: Heat a stick of unsalted butter in a heavy saucepan over low heat until it melts. Continue to let it simmer until the foam stops rising to the surface. Remove from the heat and skim off the foam, then pour the rest of the butter through a few layers of cheesecloth into a heatproof jar. Clarified butter can keep, covered, for 3 months in the refrigerator.

## Milk

Unless otherwise noted, I use whole milk in all the recipes.

## Flours

I typically use only flours milled from wheat. What makes wheat flours differ is the kind of wheat they are milled from, how they are milled, and even when and where the wheat was harvested. But for the home baker, knowing how much protein is in a flour is most important because protein determines how much gluten can be formed when dough is worked. Gluten is what gives baked goods their structure. It's easy to understand: A lot of protein makes for a strong, dense structure (breads). Lower protein content makes for a lighter, airier structure (cakes). The exact percentage of protein in a particular flour can vary by brand and country of origin, but here are the general guidelines:

**Bread Flour / 14 to 16% protein**
A strong flour I use for a variety of crusty breads, pizza dough, and rolls.

**All-Purpose (AP) Flour / 10 to 12% protein**
This is the flour I use for all sorts of baking, from cakes and pastries to breads.

**Pastry Flour / 9% protein**
Just a little stronger than cake flour, this should be used for muffins, cookies, biscuits, and soft yeast dough.

**Cake Flour / 7 to 8% protein**
A finely textured, soft flour used for delicate cakes and pastries.

# equipment check

**I've found that heavy duty, restaurant-quality baking sheets and cake pans produce even heat and promote even browning. Look for the heaviest, best quality pans you can find. Here's what I keep in my kitchen.**

## Rimmed Baking Sheets

I use them for so many things—cookies, scones, jellyroll cakes, biscuits, free-form tarts, and roasted vegetables. I even turn them over and bake my pizzas and breads on the bottom.

## Tart Pans

Always with a removable bottom for me. Always. It's so much easier to pop out the tart.

## Cake Pans

I use heavy-duty nonstick pans in every size and side height imaginable.

## Muffin Tins

I like to use the restaurant-size, heavy-duty nonstick tins that yield two dozen muffins. I double my recipes and share with friends.

## Drying racks

Mine are colorful and fit perfectly into a baking sheet.

## Pie Plates

I always use a rimmed Pyrex dish. Why? I just love the way they look. I don't think they bake any better than a metal pie tin—it's all about the rim for me. The Pyrex dishes make it easier to do fancy crimping on your pie crusts.

## Stand Mixer

I use my stand mixer for almost everything! It's the one small appliance that sits out on my counter (and that's saying a lot because I can't function around clutter—I don't even like the word "clutter"). Because it sits out on my kitchen counter, I painted Paul Smith stripes on it—don't tell Kitchen-Aid. Sure I could use my hands to knead the dough recipes, and I encourage you to use yours if you like, but I'd rather spend all my time wanting instead of kneading.

## Hand Mixer

Great as a backup to your stand mixer. Mine even has a dough hook attachment. Mostly, I use my hand mixer for whipping cream or frostings.

# conversion chart

### all conversions are approximate

## Volume Conversions

| U.S. | Metric |
|---|---|
| 1 tsp | 5 ml |
| 1 tbs | 15 ml |
| 2 tbs | 30 ml |
| 3 tbs | 45 ml |
| ¼ cup | 60 ml |
| ⅓ cup | 75 ml |
| ⅓ cup + 1 tbs | 90 ml |
| ⅓ cup + 2 tbs | 100 ml |
| ½ cup | 120 ml |
| ⅔ cup | 150 ml |
| ¾ cup | 180 ml |
| ¾ cup + 2 tbs | 200 ml |
| 1 cup | 240 ml |
| 1 cup + 2 tbs | 275 ml |
| 1¼ cups | 300 ml |
| 1⅓ cups | 325 ml |
| 1½ cups | 350 ml |
| 1⅔ cups | 375 ml |
| 1¾ cups | 400 ml |
| 1¾ cups + 2 tbs | 450 ml |
| 2 cups (1 pint) | 475 ml |
| 2 ½ cups | 600 ml |
| 3 cups | 720 ml |
| 4 cups (1 quart) | 945 ml |
| | (1,000 ml is 1 liter) |

## Weight Conversions

| U.S./U.K. | Metric |
|---|---|
| ½ oz | 14 g |
| 1 oz | 28 g |
| 1½ oz | 43 g |
| 2 oz | 57 g |
| 2½ oz | 71 g |
| 3 oz | 85 g |
| 3½ oz | 100 g |
| 4 oz | 113 g |
| 5 oz | 142 g |
| 6 oz | 170 g |
| 7 oz | 200 g |
| 8 oz | 227 g |
| 9 oz | 255 g |
| 10 oz | 284 g |
| 11 oz | 312 g |
| 12 oz | 340 g |
| 13 oz | 368 g |
| 14 oz | 400 g |
| 15 oz | 425 g |
| 1 lb | 454 g |

## Oven Temperatures

| Gas Mark | °F | °C |
|---|---|---|
| ½ | 250 | 120 |
| 1 | 275 | 140 |
| 2 | 300 | 150 |
| 3 | 325 | 165 |
| 4 | 350 | 180 |
| 5 | 375 | 190 |
| 6 | 400 | 200 |
| 7 | 425 | 220 |
| 8 | 450 | 230 |
| 9 | 475 | 240 |
| 10 | 500 | 260 |
| Broil | 550 | 290 |

**Libbie Summers** (above left) first earned her culinary chops below deck as a chef on private yachts—honing her baking skills under extreme weather and guest conditions. Today, Summers is an award-winning producer of imaginative lifestyle content for print and film clients including *Condé Nast Traveler, Bon Appétit, Huffington Post, Gilt, Southern Living,* and Paramount Pictures. Her blog Salted and Styled (cocreated with photographer Chia Chong) won the 2013 Best Food Blog award from the International Association of Culinary Professionals. *The New York Times* called her first book, *The Whole Hog Cookbook,* "aggressively pretty," while *Bon Appétit* lauded its "wicked sense of humor." Summers maintains her body and body of work are both food inspired. She lives in Savannah, Georgia, with one husband, one son, and one opinionated dog. libbiesummers.com

Chia Chong (above right) is a photographer whose diverse body of work includes food, portraiture, lifestyle, interior design, fine art, and travel. Her images have appeared in many leading publications including *Vogue, Bon Appétit, Cosmopolitan, Elle Décor, National Geographic Traveler,* and *The New York Times.* Her books include *A House in the South, Perfect Porches,* and *The Whole Hog Cookbook.* She is the co-creator with Libbie Summers of the blog Salted and Styled. Chong grew up in Penang, Malaysia, earned her BFA in Photography from Savannah College of Art and Design, and currently resides in Savannah with her husband and two daughters. chiachong.com

Jennifer S. Muller is owner and principal of Jennifer Muller Design, in Portland, Maine, where she lives with her (very sweet) son and her (not-at-all vicious) dog. She has designed logos for a popcorn cart in Brooklyn and a northern Indian take-out place in the West Village, and books about cooking for men and boys (*Mad Hungry, How to Feed Men and Boys*), cooking for Southern gatherings (*Summerland*), and cooking with pigs (*The Whole Hog Cookbook*). Her work has won awards from people who know about such things (*Communication Arts, Graphis,* Society of Publication Designers, Type Directors Club). She is probably baking a cake right now. jennifermullerdesign.com

# credits

Barrera Productions *video production* barreraproductions.com

Bastille Metal Works *pewter and zinc countertops* bastillemetalworks.com

Bethesda Academy *farm and gardens* bethesdaacademy.org

The Butcher *custom tattoo design* whatisthebutcher.com

Cheap Cookie Cutters *mini cowboy, hand, foot, and pig cookie cutters* cheapcookiecutters.com

Habersham Antiques Market *photo styling prop house* habershamantiquesmarket.com

Jessica Duthu *costume design* jessicaduthu.com

Katherine Sandoz *custom artwork* katherinesandoz.com

Matt Hebermehl *custom artwork "Get ill with my art skill"* hebermehl.com

Meddin Studios *digital media production studio* meddinstudios.com

Motorini Vespa Savannah *Vespa scooter rental and sales* vespasavannah.com

Re-Think Design Studio *branding and interior design* rethinkdesignstudio.com

24e Design Co. *custom contemporary furniture and design* 24estyle.com

shopSCAD *handmade jewelry* shopSCAD.com

SweetDejaVu *edible gold crowns* etsy.com/shop/SweetDejaVu

The Webstaurant Store *baking supplies* webstaurantstore.com

# Acknowledgments

With my first book, the people I worked with were ridiculously talented colleagues. By the time this delicious second book, *Sweet & Vicious,* was finished, I considered those same people something much greater: my friends. Friends—the most lofty word in my heart and in my vocabulary. Friends will tell you when something you wrote wasn't funny, when you aren't as skinny as you think you are in a photo, when a cake you baked "could be a lot better," and when a photo you styled was . . . and I quote . . . "hideous." I'd like to introduce you to my friends. The talented group of people who worked tirelessly to make *Sweet & Vicious* so very special and to make me laugh. I could never thank you enough for being in my life and being you. I am filled with pride with the mere keystroke of your names.

**Chia Chong, photographer.** Your talent is endless. Every day I get to work with you is extraordinary, and I couldn't have imagined doing this project with anyone else. Thank you for raising the creative bar and always inspiring me. I know you don't want to hear this, but I adore you . . . so deal with it.

**Jennifer Muller, designer.** You are a beautiful petite raven-haired magician. I handed you a pile of recipes, stories, images, and colors and you turned it all into a showy sugary rainbow. I walked on air each time you told me one of my stories made you laugh or you loved a photo. Thank you for your boundless design talents, wicked sense of humor, integrity, honesty, and love of fabric.

**Christopher Steighner, senior editor at Rizzoli International Publications.** *Sweet & Vicious* was your genius idea— your baby. Thank you for entrusting its care to me over lunch in Manhattan one winter day. What began as a cute child became a bad-ass adult beauty with the help of your intellect, thoughtfulness, and careful nudging.

**Rizzoli International Publications, publisher.** When I step off the elevator at 300 Park Avenue South, I feel like a homecoming queen. Thank you to the dapper Charles Miers for assembling a dream team of Jennifer Pierson, Jessica Napp, and Pam Sommers to promote this attitude-filled, beautiful book of baking and belly aching. And for making my head swell every time I see the fancy "R" on the spine of my books.

**Janice Shay, editor and book packager.** Your attentive help and guidance with this project kept my writing focused and on track. And, because you are so talented, you seemed to do it with ease and without ever changing my tenor (just my grammar and occasional potty mouth). Thank you for being in my corner when those calls to New York had to be made and for laughing at my stories. You are the greatest.

**Liana Krissoff, copy editor.** When you changed one of my descriptive words to the word "classy" (one of my most hated words), I had my reservations. Boy, was I wrong . . . you are a brilliant recipe copy editor and I would never call you "classy" . . . you are way too wonderful for that. Thank you for every measurement you questioned and every comma you added.

**Lauren Brown Hopkins, publicist.** You are a tiger wrapped up in a beautiful princess's body. Thank you for working hard to support my dreams, for always making me smile, and not talking too much about children around me.

**Brenda Anderson, bestie.** You tested recipes, washed dishes, cooked for days, sent cards of encouragement, and even fried up your World's Best Onion Rings for a dockside private celebration when the book photography was finished. Thank you for being a true friend and being such a light in my life and everyone's life you touch. I love you.

**Anna Heritage, personal assistant and girl wonder.** Thank you for your energy, excitement, creativity, and social media skills— I just wish you could cook. It was a blessing having you work on this project. I can't wait to see what life has in store for you and what you have in store for life.

**Eliza Barrera, videographer.** I had a dream of having an online video element to this book that was entertaining, fun, and food-inspired. Thank you for your talents in helping to bring the dream to life and for turning the audio off during B-roll gossip and smack talk.

**Anthony Lunsmann, you.** Remember when you were ten and I taught you to bake bread on a boat? Now you are a master of a grill and a master of making me smile. I love you.

**Bob and Ginger Patrick, parents.** Thank you to the two who brought me into this world and reminded me often how easy it would be to take me out.

Drumroll, please . . . In testing recipes and styling shots, I was supported by some of the best, brightest, and most sweet and vicious in the business. I am indebted to you all. Big candy-coated kisses to **Val Sivyakov, David Busch, Nancy Assuncao, Matt Baldwin, Brooke Atwood, Katherine Sandoz, Matt Hebermehl, Jules De Jesus Fritz, Paul Bailey, Jenny Long, Kimberly Padgett-Nowell, Krysti Datel, Kay Heritage, Ho Shim Shaw, Reed** and **Ellie Mae Sieving, Christopher** and **Katiana Plummer, Jeff Notrica, Dan Busey, Juwan Platt, Mary Britton Senseney, Jessica Duthu, Chris, Staci,** and **Anne Chaddock Donegan, Joel Snayd, Erica Kelly, Mitchell Hall, Jamie Deen, Ray Goto, Michael Cournoyer, Joseph Tully, Ben Fink, Cedric Smith, Nick Gant, Ruel Joyner,** and **The Bitch—Maggie Jo Summers.**

Finally, thank you, **Joshua,** for your unwavering love and support during this second book project. For making me laugh until I nearly pee my pants, forcing me to get up from watching reality shows to finish my work, and always saving me the black jelly beans. I will forever be in love with you—your crystal blue eyes and your facial-hair-free kisser.

\*

First published in the United States of America in 2014
by Rizzoli International Publications, Inc.
300 Park Avenue South, New York, NY 10010
www.rizzoliusa.com

Photographs © 2014 Chia Chong

Design and illustration by Jennifer S. Muller

2014 2015 2016 2017 / 10 9 8 7 6 5 4 3 2 1

Distributed in the U.S. trade by Random House, New York

Printed in China

ISBN-13: 978-0-8478-4104-2

Library of Congress Control Number: 2013952894

\*